Opera
Guide

Peter Grimes
Gloriana
Britten

'And God have mercy upon me!' Peter Pears as Grimes and Joan Cross as Ellen in the 1945 World première of 'Peter Grimes' (photo: Angus McBean)

Preface

This series, published under the auspices of English National Opera and The Royal Opera, aims to help audiences to enjoy and evaluate opera performances. This particular book is an introduction to two masterworks that testify to the importance of English as a language for opera. Its publication is supported by the Friends of ENO and the U.S. Friends of ENO Inc. to mark the establishment of a cultural exchange between the U.S. and the U.K. for the performance of opera in English.

Nicholas John
Series Editor

Peter Grimes
Gloriana

Benjamin Britten

Opera Guide Series Editor: Nicholas John

Published in association with
English National Opera and The Royal Opera
and sponsored by
the Friends of ENO and the US Friends of ENO Inc.

John Calder · London
Riverrun Press · New York

First published in Great Britain, 1983, by
John Calder (Publishers) Ltd,
18 Brewer Street,
London W1R 4AS

and

First published in the U.S.A., 1983, by
Riverrun Press Inc.,
175 Fifth Avenue,
New York, NY 10010

ALL RIGHTS RESERVED
BRITISH LIBRARY CATALOGUING IN PUBLICATION DATA
Britten, Benjamin
   Peter Grimes; and, Gloriana.—(Opera guide; 24)
   1. Britten, Benjamin. Peter Grimes
   2. Britten, Benjamin. Gloriana
   3. Operas—Librettos
   I. Title   II. Slater, Montagu
   III. Crabbe, George   IV. Plomer, William
   V. John, Nicholas   VI. Series
   782.1'092'4   ML410.B/

   ISBN 0-7145-3865-6
   Library of Congress Catalogue Card Number 83-045248

SUBSIDISED BY THE
Arts Council
OF GREAT BRITAIN

John Calder (Publishers) Ltd., English National Opera and
The Royal Opera House, Covent Garden Ltd., receive
financial assistance from the Arts Council of Great Britain.
English National Opera also receives financial assistance from
the Greater London Council.

Typeset in Plantin by Margaret Spooner Typesetting, Dorchester, Dorset

Printed and bound in Great Britain at The Camelot Press Ltd, Southampton

Contents

List of Illustrations

The photographs by Angus McBean are © the Harvard Theatre Museum, and are reproduced with permission.

The portraits of Elizabeth I and of Strachey are reproduced by courtesy of the Trustees of the National Portrait Gallery, and that of Plomer by courtesy of the artist.

Many of these illustrations were researched by Charles Pitt for an exhibition devoted to Benjamin Britten when *Peter Grimes* was first given at the Paris Opéra in 1981.

Benjamin Britten's Librettos

Peter Porter

Of the three elements which make up an opera — the music, the words and the drama — the third arises from the first two realised by the performance of the singing actors, with the collaboration of the musicians and within the ambience of the set and the costumes. Criticism may devote itself to an actual performance; analysis, both musical and dramatic, can be done away from the theatre, by an examination of the score. For both, the words must be considered. One sort of examination, however, is almost impossible: consideration of the book of the opera as a text in its own right. Opera librettos, as Hans Keller has written, should never be discussed away from the music they have helped to bring into existence.

There are some texts which break this rule — W.S. Gilbert's for the Savoy Operas and the books of Broadway Musicals, such as those by Lorenz Hart, Cole Porter and Ira Gerschwin. Their lyrics stand up as poems, good light verse in their own right. But operas, whether their texts are well-written in the conventional literary sense or not, have almost no value as plays, and their librettos make only a shadowy sense away from their music. Consider *Le Nozze di Figaro* (*The Marriage of Figaro*). Generations of music lovers have admired Lorenzo da Ponte's brilliant adaptation of Beaumarchais's original prose comedy, rejoicing in the skill with which the librettist has provided Mozart with a vehicle for his overwhelming genius, not least in those two miraculous finales, to Acts Two and Four, where formality of design goes hand in hand with the dramatic unfolding of the story, inspiring the composer to create some of his most complex structures. Yet the text of *Figaro* is conventional poetry, and, from the point of view of a theatregoer interested in Beaumarchais's ideas, not a patch on the play. Thus the best libretto ever written for the best opera ever written is scarcely tolerable as reading matter. Da Ponte's genius lies in his serving Mozart's genius.

What then can one proclaim about the book of any opera? And how does a good libretto from a bad one? The answer is in the music. You can go so far as to say that any words which produce good music constitute a good libretto. But the example of Handel's operas and Weber's *Euryanthe* give one pause. The convention of the Handelian *opera seria* has corroded so that today we find it frigid entertainment, but was it ever a satisfactorily dramatic form, with its succession of *da capo* arias, its wastelands of recitative, and its statuesque indifference to tension, beyond conspiracy and complication? It produced concerts of fine music, and, sometimes, as when Handel was drawn to 'magic' subjects — his Ariosto operas, *Alcina, Ariodante* and *Orlando* — words of striking, if not truly dramatic, impact. But it lacked the breath of life, which real and worldly characters give to musical drama. Handel's *Giulio Cesare* (*Julius Caesar*) is dead in the way that Monteverdi's *L'Incoronazione di Poppea* (*The Coronation of Poppea*) is not, even though the Handel work offers a story as racy as Shaw's *Caesar and Cleopatra*. The librettist's convention has spoiled it.

So we must change our definition to read — a good opera book is one which produces good dramatic music. Perhaps this is what is wrong with *Euryanthe*. Romantic attitudes were natural to writers and composers of the early 19th century, but the distance between attitudinising in words based on a great dramatic notion (*Der Freischütz*) and hollow fustian (*Euryanthe*) is all-important.

After this preamble, the question is, where did Benjamin Britten, the latest if not the last of the great composers of opera in a line stretching over three and a half centuries, look for inspiration to invent his masterpieces? What kind of librettos did he receive from his collaborators? A composer is haunted by certain themes, subjects or moods, and he must look around for the stories or dramatic vehicles he needs to bring these themes to life as musical theatre. By the time Britten began to write operas, at the start of the 1940s, the task was a formidable one. The operatic tradition, never strong in England, had weakened everywhere. It was especially out of favour with the rising avant-garde. Mozart may have sorted through hundreds of librettos discontentedly and only produced his masterpieces after finding a poet able to construct the libretto he needed, but, in his apprentice years, he had set the standard texts of the professional theatre hacks. Da Ponte was just such a professional himself, though a highly superior one. Rossini set the words of his theatre librettists happily and so, give or take a few personal quiddities, did the Italian composers of the 19th century, Verdi included. Verdi tended to choose the stories, outline and then dictate the treatment, but he handed over the actual versification to Piave, Ghislanzoni, Boito and the rest. Wagner and Berlioz went their own way and, significantly, wrote their own words. Britten's contemporary, Michael Tippett, has constructed his own texts. But the professional librettists — the so-called 'poets' of the 18th-century court theatres, such as Metastasio, and those of the 19th century, epitomised by Felice Romani, have no equivalent today, outside Tin Pan Alley and Broadway. Tippett turned down Auden as a possible collaborator. It's a matter for conjecture whether he would have been willing to accept a real theatre wordsmith had one been available.

There is one shining example of a literary man willing, with however many fastidious reservations, to collaborate with a composer — Hugo von Hofmannsthal, whose series of librettos for Richard Strauss, from *Elektra* to *Arabella*, is the most distinguished collaboration of an established poet and a famous composer since Busenello wrote for Monteverdi. A highly sophisticated and well-read composer such as Britten could be expected to look for his own Hofmannsthal. Interestingly enough, Britten did so initially, but soon turned to quite other directions.

Britten's first librettist was W.H. Auden, later to become Hofmannsthal's successor as prime librettist of the age, with operatic books written, in collaboration with Chester Kallman, for Stravinsky (*The Rake's Progress*) and Hans Werner Henze (*Elegy for Young Lovers*, *The Bassarids*). Auden's influence on the young Britten was enormous: it shaped his whole attitude to the setting of words. Britten is a vocal composer *par excellence*, and he learned, under Auden's powerful didactic spirit, much that was to bear fruit in his years as a mature artist. Although this influence is too big a subject to be discussed here, one aspect of it is vital to any consideration of Britten's operas. The operetta, *Paul Bunyan*, which Auden and Britten mounted in New York in 1941 was a bitterly disappointing experience for Britten. Whether or not he was right in thinking that he had allowed his music to be led by and all but overwhelmed by Auden's words *Paul Bunyan* marked the end of his close collaboration with Auden. Late in life, Britten thought better of his first operatic venture but, at the time, it made him determined to escape from Auden's artistic and personal domination. Never again would Britten allow a

The composer, at the piano, plays through the score of 'Peter Grimes' to Kenneth Green (designer), Eric Crozier (producer) and Reginald Goodall (conductor) on the set at Sadler's Wells in 1945. (photo: Angus McBean)

writer to be the more powerful partner in a musical collaboration. All the operas on which his world reputation are based are entirely his in idea, inspiration, lay-out and dramatic emphasis. His librettists whether poets, novelists, producers or scholars, tailored their books to his minutely worked-out requirements. None, not even literary men of distinction in their own right, like E.M. Forster, Ronald Duncan and William Plomer, showed him the way or disputed his paramountcy. Thus the qualities, including the faults and limitations of language and notion in some of the operas, are Britten's responsibility completely. People showered unsought librettos on him all his life and he ignored them. He may have taken up ideas for operas put to him by collaborators — Myfanwy Piper remembers that she first suggested the Henry James story, *The Turn of the Screw*, as a suitable subject — but the signal to proceed came from him alone. As much as Verdi, Britten is the originator of his own operatic texts.

The governing principle, therefore, in Britten's operas is the musico-dramatic thrust, and the words he set to bring the opera about are stepping-stones to the final product. I think it is sensible to separate his many librettos into categories — not for the sake of ultimate classification, but because it helps to understand the nature of the finished works, in their full musical dress. Britten's taste in opera and his forms are generally traditional, though this means nothing beyond a few observable lineaments. It does not tell us how his music works. After *Bunyan*, he is not a pioneer of operatic form until we come to the three Church Parables. I state this knowing that, in practical terms, the foundation of the English Opera Group and the composition of chamber operas of manageable proportions, such as *The Rape of Lucretia*, *Albert Herring* and *The Turn of the Screw*, look pretty initiatory. But it is not in the forces involved that I would locate the main divide in Britten's operas. The real difference is observable in the breakdown of scenes and the manner in which Britten chooses to deploy the dramatic action. The three Piper operas represent a different vision of musical dramaturgy to the rest of the Britten canon. *The Turn of the Screw, Owen Wingrave*, and *Death in Venice* are cinematic in technique in the sense that they evolve by the quick promotion and melding of short scenes. Each comes from a prose story or novella, and

9

concentrates on a sequence of sharply and economically presented emotional points, eschewing the larger structures of tension usually encountered in operas based on the dramatic convention of acts and scenes. There is no real need for any of the Piper operas to be divided into acts, least of all *Owen Wingrave*, which was created for television. Curiously, there are few parallels for this, a natural enough way of making an opera, when the librettist and composer are dealing with a narrative not already shaped into theatrical scenes. Berg's *Wozzeck* is one forerunner, but Britten and Mrs Piper deserve the accolade of being unconscious innovators. The two masterpieces of their collaboration, *The Turn of the Screw* and *Death in Venice*, have a wonderful appropriateness of form to subject. Each is a tightening or turning of the screw as, scene by scene, the action brings its dénouement closer. Brevity was always Britten's motto, as well as Verdi's. Of these two operas, the one is a remarkable spiral set of variations on a theme, and the other, a sort of whirlpool of thematic reference and counter-reference. Their style is right for obsessional subjects. You feel that the music carries the words along on the back of its urge to secure release. The innovation is not noticeable verbally. Only the complete work turns up new ground.

But if the Piper operas and, in another way, the Church Parables, are special categories within Britten's chorus of operas — what about the rest of his output, which contains his better-known creations? They are all 'Act and Scene' operas — their librettos organised along familiar lines, those analogous to the partitioning of dramatic action usual on the non-musical stage, where soliloquy, dialogue, ensemble, and purely mimed material add up to a whole dramatic structure. Certainly each inhabits its own world, and they all differ from each other. *The Rape of Lucretia*, for instance, is encased within a Christian commentary provided by a male and female narrator. *A Midsummer Night's Dream* is a brilliant biopsy of the play, where Britten's music miraculously replaces Shakespeare's poetry without damaging the original drama. Even *Billy Budd*, which seems on the face of it the most orthodox — that is the most like the 19th-century Grand Opera — is unusual in having no part for a female voice, and *Albert Herring* has elements of Gilbert and Sullivan in it, not least in the cunningly-written farcical libretto.

This leaves *Gloriana* and *Peter Grimes*, the subjects of this book, to be considered. *Gloriana* is much less familiar than *Grimes*, and I shall approach it first. Elsewhere contributors will deal with the circumstances of *Gloriana*'s creation, and the unfavourable reception it had during the Coronation Festivities in 1953. I intend to consider the libretto as Britten's realistic reaction to a story that was all too easy to render as either full-blown Grand Opera or stagey High Camp. Examples of the first sort were there to warn him before he began in Schiller's *Mary Stuart* and Donizetti's relatively ineffective *Maria Stuarda*, plus dozens of other representations of Tudor History and the Virgin Queen in opera, novel and film. Britten includes Sir Walter Raleigh as a character in *Gloriana*. Raleigh, sung by a bass, is shown as dignified, even pompous, slightly resentful of the aspirations of younger courtiers such as Mountjoy and the Earl of Essex. Britten invests him with a memorable sententiousness of utterance, something one might call proverbial if such a word could apply to a melodic line. His music stems from the same shaping hand as that which invented the Voice of God in Britten's second canticle *Abraham and Isaac*, composed just before *Gloriana*. 'When head and heart are hot / Then tongue and hand are wild: / So, Ma'am, it looks to me', Raleigh replies when the Queen asks him what he thinks of the dispute between Essex and Mountjoy, and the last line is set with a homely finality which reminds us that, by the end of Gloriana's reign, Raleigh is no longer a young man, and that the historic Raleigh had a taste for literary homily, as in his poem 'The Lie'. Nothing could be further from costume drama or the spreading of cloaks over puddles.

Still, that first audience was not wrong in noticing something unusual in *Gloriana*. It is an opera of the romance of truthfulness. Britten and William Plomer, his librettist, must have known instinctively that an opera celebrating the most masterful sovereign in English history nevertheless could not offer a modern (even a Coronation) audience Good Queen Bess or Schiller's avenging spitfire. It was the glory of the realm which could go into music: that and the triumphant regality of an old, vain woman. They therefore devised no conventional love interest. Essex loves the Queen since she is the embodiment of England. With Lytton Strachey's *Elizabeth and Essex* as their source, they invented scenes which would open out the twin deltas of their story: Elizabeth the monarch and Elizabeth the woman. The opera was to be half a triumphant progress of a great queen through history (and how appropriate that it should contain, in Act Two, a Royal Progress), and half a story of an old woman disappointed by a selfish man. The two themes converge in the final act, when the Queen is faced with the warrant for Essex's execution. Her hesitation is filled with pathos, but the opera's other vein of emotion dictates the sacrifice of an indulgence for the welfare of her country. Plomer and Britten did not attempt any Verdian tug of love and duty, as will be found in *Don Carlos*. *Gloriana* is a pageant opera, but it shows us the heartbreak behind the painted progress. It is at an opposite pole to *The Turn of the Screw*, where every detail advances the tragedy. Thus the last scene, with the Queen's death, and the recollection of the glories of her reign, is not irrelevant. Essex was never more than the human relaxation of Elizabeth's supreme call to duty. Her love was always for her people, and the quotations from her historic speeches (which are not set to music) represent her carefully-chosen communications to them. Death, of course, lays its icy hand on kings, as on other men, and Elizabeth's remonstrance against Essex is proclaimed in the thunderous recapitulation of his lute song. The opera was twinned in themes from the start, and it remains so, even after the one theme of individual love is sacrificed.

The text of *Gloriana* is finely literate, but it is not literature. It would be exceeding its purposes if it were. William Plomer, writer of some of the best light satires in modern English and a happily ironic novelist, is never tempted to bring his own genius forward at the expense of dramatic necessity. A composer adds music to the basic shapes of language as a poet adds poetry to notions. Therefore poetry on its own is out of place in a libretto. Nevertheless, Plomer shows a fine ear for the dramatic exchanges of his story: his half-rhymes are as just as his formal pieces — songs, homilies and ballads. The choral dances from the Norwich scene are often performed in concert and are widely admired. Plomer's words for this formal masque are nicely dry and traditional: there is none of that damply effulgent poetry which is so damaging in Ronald Duncan's verse for *The Rape of Lucretia*. Above all, Plomer merely touches on the Elizabethan cadence and diction. His text hints at the periods and utterances of Gloriana's England, but it quite avoids the 'half-timbered'. The second lute song, Essex's own poem, does not stand out unduly. The libretto is the true counterpart of Britten's music for the ball scene (Act Two, scene three), where period inflexions and cadences stop short of pastiche. The scene of Essex's rebellion, in which the Earl never appears, has been judged unfavourably, especially the running commentary provided by the blind ballad-singer. I wonder how widely praised this scene would be if it had issued

11

Balstrode (Roderick Jones), Auntie (Edith Coates) and the Nieces (Blanche Turner, Minnia Bowers) in the pub (1945, Sadler's Wells) (photo: Angus McBean)

from the hands of Brecht or one of his collaborators. In general, the action in Plomer's drama is neither wilful nor shrinking. It is just different from what it would be had *Gloriana* been intended as a Grand Opera in the *Aida* sense. Instead, it is an opera about the genius of England, and about the vicissitudes, at the end of a long and glorious reign, of one of England's most loved and applauded worthies. Perhaps the chorus of the English people, which its wide-arching melody and plangent harmonising, sums up the whole work. As a piece of poetry, it seems a fairly conventional summoning of royal emblems. Heard in the opera, it is tinged with love and sadness:

> Green leaves are we,
> Red rose our golden Queen,
> O crownèd rose among the leaves so green!

*

Peter Grimes is so famous it runs the risk of being taken for some sort of operatic norm. It is, rather, a very singular opera, like no other. That it made both Britten's reputation and, at one stroke, recreated opera in English, a lost cause since the days of Purcell, is today almost a hedge to our seeing it clearly. For a start *Grimes* is peculiar in being derived from a poem, or a set of poems — George Crabbe's omnibus portrait of *The Borough*, a sort of demographic survey of Aldeburgh, on the Suffolk coast, at the beginning of the 19th century. Britten happened upon an article about Crabbe, the most English of poets and the most local, by E.M. Forster in *The Listener*, while homesick in California in 1941. Armed with a commission for an opera from the Koussevitzky Foundation, Britten enlisted the aid of Montagu Slater in making an opera about his native demesne, the fishing villages of East Suffolk. It is only rarely that places become the heroes of operas, yet such is the case of *Peter Grimes*. The opera is first and foremost an evocation of *genius loci*, and subsequently a gallery of types and humours. It stands directly in the line of great folk operas, such as Verdi's *La Forza del Destino (The Force of Destiny)* and Mussorgsky's *Boris Godunov*, and, like them, it makes a great play with the chorus as a

Auntie (Edith Coates) consoles Ellen (Joan Cross) (1945, Sadler's Wells) (photo: Angus McBean)

centre of passion. I stress this folk opera strength in *Grimes*, because it is usually considered an example of the doom of the individual, faced by the oppression of society. Although it is true that Grimes is seen by Crabbe and by Slater and Britten as an outsider figure, he is no typical tragic hero. His fate, as shown by both poet and librettist, is almost foredoomed, and on his struggle they hang the themes of the harsh life of the fishing community, and the power of an indifferent Nature, moulding all men, conformists and rebels alike, to rituals of accommodation. Almost everything in *Peter Grimes* is superbly realised by the music, except the character of Peter himself. Yet the miracle of Britten's score is that this does not injure the effect of the whole work. Our noses are simply pointed in other directions.

Montagu Slater worked from Crabbe's many detailed portraits of Aldeburgh's denizens to fashion his libretto. There is a mass of couplets itemising the Vicar, the Curate, the Clubs and Social Meetings, Inns, Almshouses etc.. Here are found almost all the characters of the opera, including Auntie the publican and her ubiquitously recruited 'nieces', Ned Keene the quack apothecary, Mrs Sedley the East-Indiaman's widow, Ellen Orford the widowed school-teacher, Bob Boles the Methodist Lay-preacher, Swallow the local magistrate, bully and lawyer, and even Dr Crabbe (a nominal intrusion) the medico. The heart of Crabbe's presentation of *The Borough* is the fisherman Peter Grimes, attaining in the midst of Crabbe's Parliamentary Blue Book couplets, a strangely 'poète maudit' character. As Crabbe describes him, Grimes begins as a brutal product of harsh circumstances. But by the end of the poem, he has become a character of extra-terrestrial proportions, a romantic sufferer carrying on his shoulders the sins of society. It was this romantic dimension which Britten set out to portray. But when he and Slater came to devise the dramatic structure of the libretto, something different resulted. The music Britten has given to Grimes is superb — obviously such pieces as 'Now the Great Bear and the Pleiades', his visionary monologue in the Pub scene, and his final exaltation of madness after the manhunt, are wonderful dramatic music by any standard — but nevertheless, Grimes's romanticism is at variance with the plot. Such difficulty is compounded by the fact that Britten wrote the part of Grimes with Peter Pears in mind. Pears is probably the best singing actor I have ever seen and heard, but the range of his abilities does not extend to playing a brutal fisherman. Pears as Captain Vere in *Billy Budd*, an equally tailor-made role, is utterly convincing. I have seen him as Grimes many times and never without a sense of embarrassment that this finely sensitive singer should have been asked to adopt a vicious role alien to him. Nor have other performances, those by Edgar Evans, Ronald Dowd and Jon Vickers, convinced me. Mozart tailored his parts to his singers. The musical personality of Grimes, devised for Pears, cannot be made to fit the character of the libretto.

In Crabbe's poem we are shown Peter deriding his dying father. Grown-up in his own fisherman's kingdom, his cruelty brands him an emblematic villain. Yet there is also a warped idealism:

> And hoped to find in some propitious hour,
> A feeling creature subject to his power.

The apprentice boys whom Grimes mistreats are attendant angels of his fallen state. His violence towards them might even be deemed no more than a Satanic desire to get them used to the notion of reigning in Hell rather than serving in Heaven. Grimes's misanthropy is a proper match for the Borough's small-minded respectability. The Borough, willing enough to disparage and hunt down Grimes, cares little for the fate of his apprentices, though Crabbe is never as explicit as Slater is in the libretto. There Balstrode, the retired sea-captain, says, 'Something of the sort befits / Brats conceived outside the sheets'. Crabbe asks rhetorically why no-one raised a hand to help Grimes's workhouse slaves, but comments that all they ever said on hearing of the children's misery was — 'Grimes is at his exercise'. This line becomes the key passage in the great scene in Act Two when, after church, the Borough is aroused to invade Grimes's hut. The ruin of Grimes inspires some of Crabbe's greatest poetry, a real vision of despair, as the fisherman, fallen into madness, finds no consolation but the contemplation of Nature at its most implacable, drifting in his boat among the unlovely reeds, mudflats and backwaters of Aldeburgh and Slaughden Quay. (These lines are quoted in Forster's article on page 16: 'When tides were neap . . .') There is no real equivalent of this poetry in Britten's opera because his gaze is directed elsewhere. Slater and Britten were writing an opera, and had to have more plot than Crabbe affords. Slater did a marvellous job, and I think this should be asserted firmly, now that both he and Britten are dead, since the composer was given to accusing his collaborator, in later days, of penning many solecisms in the text of *Peter Grimes*. The libretto is an extremely skilful composition of short lines, dotted with half-rhymes, traditional sayings and vernacular turns of language. It is neither quite verisimilitudinous, nor unnecessarily poetic: it accommodates all the many Borough characters without strain. It is as though Crabbe's personal inspiration, which surrounds Grimes with a visionary nimbus, becomes one part of the opera, and the whole series of poems which make up *The Borough* become the rest of the opera. Slater provided Britten with pen-portraits out of Crabbe which can never be forgotten once they are encountered. The superb choruses, picking up as they do lines from various Crabbe poems, inherit the point-of-view of his editorial stoicism. This is what Kipling called 'England . . . on the anvil', and the character of Peter Grimes, is the centre around which so much of this English genius revolves. It is appropriate that the first great English opera of modern times should be so deeply English in tone, and should derive from the art which the English have always excelled at — poetry.

George Crabbe: The Poet and the Man

E.M. Forster

To think of Crabbe is to think of England. He never left our shores and he only once ventured to cross the border into Scotland. He did not even go to London much, but lived in villages and small country towns. He was a clergyman of the English Church. His Christian name was that of our national saint. Moreover, his father was also called George, and so was his grandfather, and he christened his eldest son George, and his grandson was called George also. Five generations of George Crabbes!

Our particular George Crabbe was born (in the year 1755) at Aldeborough, on the coast of Suffolk. It is a bleak little place; not beautiful. It huddles round a flint-towered church and sprawls down to the North Sea — and what a wallop the sea makes as it pounds at the shingle! Near by is a quay, at the side of an estuary, and here the scenery becomes melancholy and flat; expanses of mud, saltish commons, the marsh-birds crying. Crabbe heard that sound and saw that melancholy and they got into his verse. He worked as an unhappy little boy on the quay, rolling barrels about and storing them in a warehouse, under orders from his father. He hated it. His mother had died: his father was cross. Now and then he got hold of a book, or looked at some prints, or chatted with a local worthy, but it was a hard life and they were in narrow circumstances. He grew up among poor people, and he has been called their poet. But he did not like the poor. When he started writing, it was the fashion to pretend that they were happy shepherds and shepherdesses, who were always dancing, or anyhow had hearts of gold. But Crabbe knew the local almshouses and the hospital and the prison, and the sort of people who drift into them; he read, in the parish registers, the deaths of the unsuccessful, the marriages of the incompetent, and the births of the illegitimate. Though he notes occasional heroism, his general verdict on the working classes is unfavourable. And when he comes to the richer and more respectable inmates of the borough who can veil their defects behind money, he remains sardonic, and sees them as poor people who have not been found out.

He escaped from Aldeborough as soon as he could. His fortunes improved, he won the patronage of Burke, took orders, married well, and ended his life in 1832 in a comfortable West Country parsonage. He had done well for himself. Yet he never escaped from Aldeborough in the spirit, and it was the making of him as a poet. Even when he was writing of other things, there steals again and again into his verse the sea, the estuary, the flat Suffolk coast, local meannesses, and an odour of brine and dirt — tempered occasionally with the scent of flowers. We must remember Aldeborough when we read this rather odd poet, for he belongs to the grim little place, and through it to England. And we must remember that though he is an Englishman, he is not a John Bull, and that though he is a clergyman, he is by no means an 'old dear'.

His poems are easily described and read. They are mostly stories in rhymed couplets, and their subject is local scenes or people. One story will be about almshouses, another about the vicar, another about inns. *Peter Grimes*, which inspires Britten's opera, had an actual original. Another story — the charming *Silford Hall* — tells of a happy visit which a little boy once paid to a country mansion, and how the kind housekeeper showed him round the picture gallery, and gave him a lovely dinner in the servants' hall; Crabbe had himself been that humble little boy. He is not brilliant or cultivated, witty or townified. He is provincial; and I am using provincial as a word of high praise.

How good are these stories in verse? Crabbe is a peculiar writer: some people like him, others don't, and find him dull and even unpleasant. I like him and read him again and again; and his tartness, his acid humour, his honesty, his feeling for certain English types and certain kinds of English scenery do appeal to me very much. On their account I excuse the absence in him of a warm heart, a vivid imagination, and a grand style: for he has none of those great gifts.

Here are some verses from *Peter Grimes*. They show how Crabbe looks at scenery, and how subtly he links the scene with the soul of the observer. The criminal Grimes is already suspected of murdering his apprentices, and no one will go fishing with him in his boat. He rows out alone into the estuary, and waits there — waits for what?

> When tides were neap, and, in the sultry day,
> Through the tall bounding mud-banks made their way . . .
> There anchoring, Peter chose from man to hide,
> There hang his head, and view the lazy tide
> In its hot slimy channel slowly glide;
> Where the small eels that left the deeper way
> For the warm shore, within the shallows play;
> Where gaping mussels, left upon the mud,
> Slope their slow passage to the fallen flood; —

How quiet this writing is: you might say how dreary. Yet how sure is its touch; and how vivid that estuary near Aldeborough.

> Here dull and hopeless he'd lie down and trace
> How sidelong crabs had scrawled their crooked race,
> Or sadly listen to the tuneless cry
> Of fishing gull or clanging golden-eye;
> What time the sea-birds to the marsh would come,
> And the loud bittern from the bulrush home,
> Gave from the salt ditch side the bellowing boom:
> He nursed the feelings these dull scenes produce,
> And loved to stop beside the opening sluice.

Not great poetry, by any means; but it convinces me that Crabbe and Peter Grimes and myself do stop beside an opening sluice, and that we are looking at an actual English tideway, and not at some vague, vast imaginary waterfall, which crashes from nowhere to nowhere.

Into this ordinariness, out of the muddy water, rise the spectres — the murdered boys, led by Grimes's father; and Crabbe, hostile to his own father, leads up to a death-bed of insanity and terror. He is not often so powerful.

> 'Still did they force me on the oar to rest,
> And when they saw me fainting and oppress'd,
> He with his hand, the old man, scoop'd the flood,
> And there came flame about him mix'd with blood:
> He bade me stoop and look upon the place,
> Then flung the hot red liquor in my face:
> Burning it blazed, and then I roar'd for pain,
> I thought the demons would have turn'd my brain.'
>   . . . But here he ceased and gazed
> On all around, affrighten'd and amazed;
> And still he tried to speak, and look'd in dread
> Of frighten'd females gathering round his bed;
> Then dropp'd exhausted, and appear'd at rest,
> Till the strong foe the vital powers possess'd;
> Then with an inward, broken voice he cried,
> 'Again they come!' and mutter'd as he died.

My next quotation is a lighter one. It comes from a malicious poem about the Vicar of the Parish 'whose constant care was no man to offend'. He begins with a sympathetic description of Aldeborough church, and its lichen-encrusted tower, and now he turns, with less sympathy, to the church's recently deceased incumbent. What a cruel account is this of the Vicar's one and only love affair! He had been attracted to a young lady who lived with her mother; he called on them constantly, smiling all the time, but never saying what he was after; with the inevitable result that the damsel got tired of her 'tortoise', and gave her hand to a brisker suitor. Thus ended the Vicar's sole excursion into the realm of passion.

> 'I am escaped,' he said, when none pursued;
> When none attack'd him, 'I am unsubdued;'
> 'Oh pleasing pangs of love!' he sang again,
> Cold to the joy, and stranger to the pain.
> E'en in his age would he address the young,
> 'I, too, have felt these fires, and they are strong;'
> But from the time he left his favourite maid,
> To ancient females his devoirs were paid:
> And still they miss him after morning prayer.

He was always 'cheerful and in season gay', he gave the ladies presents of flowers from his garden with mottoes attached; he was fond of fishing, he organized charades, he valued friendship, but was not prepared to risk anything for it. One thing did upset him, and that was innovation; if the Vicar discovered anything new, on either the theological or the social horizon, he grew hot — it was the only time he did get hot.

> Habit with him was all the test of truth:
> 'It must be right; I've done it from my youth.'
> Questions he answer'd in as brief a way:
> 'It must be wrong — it was of yesterday.'
> Though mild benevolence our priest possess'd,
> 'Twas but by wishes or by words express'd.
> Circles in water, as they wider flow,
> The less conspicuous in their progress grow,
> And when at last they touch upon the shore,
> Distinction ceases, and they're view'd no more.
> His love, like that last circle, all embraced,
> But with effect that never could be traced.

The Vicar's fault is weakness, and the analysis and censure of weakness is a speciality of Crabbe's. His characters postpone marriage until passion has died; perhaps this was his own case, and why he was so bitter about it. Or they marry, and passion dies because they are too trivial to sustain it. Or they drift into vice, and do even that too late, so that they are too old to relish the lustiness of sin. Or like the Vicar they keep to the straight path because vice is more arduous than virtue. To all of them, and to their weaknesses, Crabbe extends a little pity, a little contempt, a little cynicism, and a much larger portion of reproof. The bitterness of his early experiences has eaten into his soul, and he does not love the human race, though he does not denounce it, and dare not despair of its ultimate redemption.

But we must get back to the Vicar, who is awaiting his final epitaph in some anxiety.

> Now rests our Vicar. They who knew him best,
> Proclaim his life t'have been entirely rest; ...
> The rich approved, — of them in awe he stood;
> The poor admired, — they all believed him good;
> The old and serious of his habits spoke;
> The frank and youthful loved his pleasant joke;
> Mothers approved a safe contented guest,
> And daughters one who back'd each small request: ...
> No trifles fail'd his yielding mind to please,
> And all his passions sank in early ease;
> Nor one so old has left this world of sin,
> More like the being that he entered in.

For the Vicar died as a child, who retains his innocence because he has never gained any experience.

These two poems, *Peter Grimes* and *The Vicar*, represent the tragic and the satirical side of Crabbe. He is never romantic. Charming at first sight is this picture of the warm-blooded sailor who sets out to win a girl because he has been told he is beneath her. But the chase ends in squalor.

> His trusty staff in his bold hand he took,
> Like him and like his frigate, heart of oak;
> Fresh were his features, his attire was new;
> Clean was his linen, and his jacket blue;
> Of finest jean his trousers, tight and trim;
> Brush'd the large buckle at the silver rim.
> He soon arrived, he traced the village green,
> There saw the maid, and was with pleasure seen;
> Then talk'd of love . . .

The sailor dies in battle, the girl is disowned of her father, the Parish Clerk enters another bastard in the Register.

> No lads nor lasses came
> To grace the rite, or give the child a name:
> Nor grave conceited nurse, of office proud,
> Bore the young Christian roaring through the crowd.
> In a small chamber was my office done . . .

Melancholy mists invade the scene. The warm blooded, like the wicked, and like the prudent, have failed.

Crabbe's personality is definitely unattractive. For this his upbringing and his epoch were partly responsible; he was not quite the gentleman, which he regretted, and Burns had not yet exempted literary men from this particular form of remorse. And he suffered from moral gaucherie also: he disapproved, he reproved. Wherever he looked, he saw human beings taking the wrong turning. This advantaged his art. Disapproval is all too common in the pulpit, but it is rare in poetry, and its presence gives his work a curious flavour, subtle yet tart, which will always attract connoisseurs. We take a bite from an unusual fruit. We come away neither nourished nor ravished, yet aware of a new experience, which we can repeat at will. Were Crabbe insincere, we should not return, but disapproval is as genuine in his hand as indignation in Carlyle's, and, like Carlyle, he never hesitates to turn his weapon against himself. An unusual atmosphere results: it is, so to speak, sub-Christian: there is an implication throughout of positive ideals, such as self-sacrifice and asceticism, but they are rarely pressed; only occasionally does the narrator let himself testify. As a rule, he prefers to shake his finger at men as they move by wrong paths from the cradle to the grave, and to remind himself with a frown that he, too, is human — a frown that is almost a sigh:

> It is a lovely place, and at the side
> Rises a mountain rock in rugged pride,
> And in that rock are shapes of shells and forms
> Of creatures in old worlds, of nameless worms,
> Whose generations lived and died ere man,
> A worm of other class, to crawl began.

A worm with an immortal soul no doubt, but he never stresses this, for his muse, like his church, discouraged enthusiasm.

Crabbe is not one of our great poets. But he is unusual, he is straight, and he is entirely of England. Aldeborough stamped him for ever. His life was written by the George Crabbe who was his son; modest, truthful, and sensitive, it is one of the best biographies in our language.

[Reprinted, with alterations and additions, from *The Listener* for May 29, 1941, in the Sadler's Wells Opera Book about *Peter Grimes*, 1945.]

A Commentary on the Music

Stephen Walsh

Like most works that are felt to mark some kind of watershed in the history of music, *Peter Grimes* has been heavily probed for, among other things, debts to and possible borrowings from the works of other composers. But the initial impression of that first-night audience in June 1945, a month after the end of the war in Europe, seems to have been that the music was above all something new, a fresh beginning, or, for those who disliked it (a fair number), a regrettable break with the English tradition. One can reasonably say that British opera-goers in 1945 knew a lot fewer works than their modern counterparts and knew them, by and large, in less good and faithful performances. Moreover, stage performances of opera had been a rarity during the war. So one can well imagine that *Grimes* blew into Sadler's Wells like an Aldeburgh gale, changing the coastline, breaking down bridges, and generally modifying the landscape by its sheer force and energy. The fact that it was profoundly a work of synthesis was obviously much less important at first, and may even seem not very important now, as one settles down to enjoy it for the first or umpteenth time.

In fact it was already a quality of Britten's music before *Grimes* that it said new things with material which, on closer inspection, often turned out to be surprisingly familiar and straightforward. One has only to think of the simple arpeggios and ostinatos based on triads in *Les Illuminations* (1939), or the seemingly effortless, tuneful setting of well-known poetry in the *Serenade* (1943). The same sort of thing is true of *Grimes* on practically every level. The freshness and novelty of the musical language can gradually be heard as a brilliant, prismatic treatment of 'old-fashioned' tonal devices refracted through two or three prevailing modal scales. Or take the word-setting and the overall flow of the dramaturgy. Their apparent naturalism, which perturbed early audiences who thought of opera either as foreign and artificial or as translated and doubly artificial, is more truly a clever new stylisation of conventional operatic procedures like recitative, aria, rhyming couplets, verse forms, linguistic conceits, and so forth. The musical form itself, notwithstanding its almost televisual 'realism' of pace, is contrived, in the best sense. In an introduction to the Sadler's Wells Opera Book on *Peter Grimes** Britten mentioned his adoption of the 'classical practice of separate numbers' and his rejection of 'the Wagnerian theory of "permanent melody"'. Neither point is as obvious on hearing as one might expect. With a couple of exceptions, the 'separate numbers' are actually inseparable from their context while, on the other hand, Britten does use Wagnerian leitmotifs as part of a rather more generalised system of motivic transformations. And the purpose of these transformations, it transpires, is to mediate between the necessity for the plot and characters to develop, and a purely musical need for form in the classical sense. Since these points are clearly illustrated by the Prologue, it might be as well to launch our discussion of the score, without more preamble, at the start of the work.

The ingredients of this court scene are typical of Britten's particular kind of naturalism. For one thing, nearly all the characters in the drama are introduced to us. But while it seems at first quite normal that this should

* *Benjamin Britten: Peter Grimes*, ed. Eric Crozier (London, 1945).

happen — at an inquest involving the opera's central character — one soon notices that the process is in fact highly artificial, like the narrations which open several of Britten's later operas, designed in this instance to have the *dramatis personae* stand up and be recognised but in a context which fits the story. None of these figures actually gives evidence, and even musically they are practically ignored. Instead the music concentrates on three characters and the thematic contrasts they suggest: the lawyer Swallow, Grimes himself, and the chorus as a kind of Mussorgskian entity, representing the Borough and popular feeling on both sides of the 'Grimes question'. The very opening theme [1], in a matter-of-fact but distinctly pompous B flat major, is Swallow's own motif, while Grimes is portrayed not by a theme but, as we shall see, by a texture. The chorus appears in two musical guises: first, a little chattering woodwind semiquaver figure [2] which greets the more startling of Grimes's revelations and Swallow's jokes ('You mean, you threw the fish overboard?'); secondly, a series of choruses in the manner of Bach's Passions accompanied by this figure. These various ideas are joined by what amounts to recitative, with speech patterns in the vocal parts, extended passages of monotone (a device Britten uses a lot in *Grimes*), and very light orchestral accompaniment including a number of silent bars. However, there is nothing 'free' about this recitative. The whole scene is composed in a strict 4/4 time broken only by two or three pauses, and every nuance of verbal rhythm, as well as pitch, is notated. This technique enables Britten to vary, in a controlled compositional way, the essential squareness and down-to-earthness appropriate to a court of law. When Grimes steps into the witness box, the veiled string texture and weary cross-rhythms in the bass tell us before he has opened his mouth that here is a man who will not fit into conventional social patterns. More prosaically, the conversational exchanges which are such a convincing aspect of the scene are achieved simply by shifting the word stress in relation to the constant pulse.

There is a corollary to this in the curious offset notes and phrases of the vocal melody which lend a kind of speech colour to the basically simple tonal language, while giving mobility to the harmony (a change of direction in an unaccompanied vocal figure may lead unceremoniously to a change of key).

Thus Britten contrives a flexible yet controlled naturalism of detail. But what is perhaps more surprising about this scene, which has about it so much of the 'well-made play', is that its form is a purely musical conception, with a closed key structure, a carefully placed recapitulation, balanced episodes and a definite coda and conclusion. Again this is a standard procedure throughout *Grimes*. These closed, self-contained forms are hardly the 'classical practice of separate numbers', though they certainly embrace elements of that practice. They are more like (while much clearer than) the formal method used by Berg in *Wozzeck* and *Lulu*, both of which use concealed forms of various kinds to brace the free symphonic flow of the music-drama. Not that Britten's

20

ROH, 1977: Mrs Sedley (Patricia Payne) and Ned Keene (Thomas Allen) (photo: Clive Barda)

Prologue is in 'sonata-form' or any other nominal academic form (though it does bear some passing resemblance to the first movement of Sibelius's Third Symphony, which *is* in sonata-form). Rather, its form is *sui generis*, tailored to the needs of the drama, but so that its musical lay-out has a pattern and logic of its own which at once support and channel the energy of the story. At this early stage, the impact of the idea is modest. But later on it will assume much greater significance as a vehicle for the dramatic thrust of the music.

It might be helpful at this point to consider how the opera as a whole works along comparable lines. Leaving aside the Prologue and the short un-accompanied duet for Peter and Ellen which links it to the first act proper, each of the three acts is prefaced by an orchestral 'interlude', and there are three more of these interludes separating the scenes within the acts. Hans Keller pointed out many years ago* that, while the three preludial 'interludes' are broadly speaking of a generic nature, setting the scene and mood for when the curtain rises, the three mid-act interludes have more specifically psychological connotations, telling us something about the state of the dramatic action and particularly about Grimes himself. As one would expect, if this analysis is correct, the role of these central interludes is also structurally decisive. The interludes at the start of each act determine the character of the music for a time (except for Interlude V, which is abruptly curtailed by the Barn Dance music of Act Three scene one, lending thereafter only a few sinister flecks of moonlight). But they soon fade into the background, leaving behind only thematic reminiscences which are picked up and swiftly developed in a manner suitable to the changing dramatic context. In each case this process culminates, both musically and dramatically, in the central interlude, and these central interludes are so powerful and momentous that the scenes which follow can only be fitted, so to speak, into their musical reverberations. One could almost say that the second scenes really belong to the interludes which precede them though in the final act Britten adds to

* In *Benjamin Britten*, ed. Mitchell and Keller (London, 1952) and the Cambridge Opera Handbook on *Peter Grimes*, ed. Philip Brett (Cambridge, 1983).

Grimes's last monologue a reprise of the first interlude, whose function is to close out the musical form of the opera as a whole.

Though it looks painfully obvious described so baldly, this scheme is wonderfully successful in dramatising the way in which life gradually closes in on Peter, driving him inexorably to madness and suicide. In the first half of each act we have a seascape followed by a variety of genre scenes interspersed with conversations, arguments, quarrels. Each time the tension starts building up round Grimes, either in his person or in his absence, and eventually the mood erupts in an orchestral interlude descriptive in some way of the horror and introspection of Grimes's existence and leading to a scene in which that existence is laid bare in monologue. But in the first of these scenes, Act One scene two, the intensity is not yet, of course, such that the monologue occupies the entire dramatic space. Instead it increases from act to act. So there is a very strong sense, produced by both the narrative and the musical design, that the mad-scene (hallowed operatic device that it is) is a truthful climax of everything that has preceded it. The final 'Dawn' sequence then has the effect both of a reprise, closing the musical form, and of an ironic comment on the human tragedy which, when it is taken out of the public arena into the privacy of Grimes's mind, actually passes out of the consciousness and memory of those who, only a few hours before, have been clamouring loudest for its execution.

Not the least remarkable thing about *Peter Grimes*, bearing in mind Britten's theatrical inexperience at the time, is his equal assurance in handling two quite different basic types of music-drama: the genre crowd-scene on the one hand, and, on the other, the monologue. With the genre scenes, part of the secret lies again in the way natural-sounding dialogue is skilfully caught up into a formal musical structure. Britten combines this with a highly resourceful method of linking and transforming themes, so that ideas which are at first simply pictorial take on a psychological meaning in the story, or vice versa. There is a fine example of this between the Peter/Ellen duet at the end of the Prologue and the well-known 'Dawn' Interlude (I) into which it leads. After the Prologue's plain B flat close, Peter slides up a semitone, B flat to C flat, on the words 'the truth', raising a question (both musical and verbal) which is then twisted, in the course of the duet, into a doubt between Ellen's optimistic E major and Peter's pessimistic F minor (a semitone above, but with the same third degree, G sharp/A flat). The same interval, extended by an octave into a minor ninth, later expresses the couple's quest for a peace beyond the agony of the present ('Your voice out of the pain . . .')

But as this music fades into the Interlude the E/F figure is suddenly no more than a detail in the seascape, a gull's cry perhaps or a slight turbulence on the water [3]. This particular idea, unpromising though it may seem when reduced to words, is put by Britten to astonishingly fruitful use in the course of the opera. Melodramatic examples, like Peter's clawing up to F sharp on the phrase 'We shall be free' while the chorus chants relentlessly on F natural (Act Two scene one), or the foghorn's mindless E flat against D on 'the tide will turn' in the last scene, hardly need pointing out to the attentive listener. Nor perhaps need one dwell on the powerful thematic use of the expanded, minor-

Covent Garden, 1977: The nieces, Teresa Cahill and Anne Pashley (photo: Clive Barda)

ninth version of the idea, especially as it expresses Grimes's insatiable yearning for 'haven', for acceptance and respect — a yearning so intimately bound up with his personal tragedy because, to most of us, these things seem comparatively within reach (whether we desire them or not) but are patently and without qualification beyond Peter's grasp: [8, 10, 17]. More subtle is the way the minor second also becomes symbolic of the Storm, again starting as a purely graphic detail. There is no mistaking the physical menace in the soft but grinding discord which announces Balstrode's 'Look, the storm cone', or the thrill of fear in his fugue theme 'Now the flood tide' [7], with its opening minor second, which is picked up by the entire chorus and worked into one of those overwhelming Verdian ensembles which climax the first scene of each act. But in the ensuing duet for Balstrode and Grimes, this motif gets so entangled with Grimes's personal strife and obstinate nature that by the time the 'Storm' interlude itself begins (with a variant of the fugue subject) we may genuinely wonder whether the hurricane is not as much an inward as an outward affair. The storm theme [11] hurls the minor second at us on various levels, but most powerfully on the root note E flat, suggesting the Phrygian mode (i.e. E to E on the white notes of the piano, transposed down a semitone). And this dark Phrygian colouring is one of the most prominent melodic and harmonic effects in the whole opera.

The Storm, as already noted, is the first of those central interludes which explode out of the tension of the preceding scenes and reach forward to control the scenes which follow. Once again Britten keeps his grip on the music with the help of a formal scheme, this time a rondo with episodes the third of which alludes directly to Grimes by quoting the two distinct themes of his phrase,

'What harbour shelters peace, away from tidal waves, away from storms' [10], followed by a pointed combination of his next theme, 'With her there'll be no quarrels', with one of the most agitated of the semitonal storm motifs (almost the next time Peter and Ellen meet on stage they do quarrel).

As the curtain rises on the interior of The Boar (Act One, scene two) we embark on the first of four scenes in which Britten frames a rapidly foward-moving dramatic action with elements of an abstract and self-generating musical form. In the present case the effect is helped by the realistic context, since the storm is still raging outside and whenever the door is opened to let in a new character the form-generating music rushes in as well in the shape of the hurricane. Although we only hear fragments of the storm, the music has such presence, and its elements are so cunningly chosen, that we can quite well imagine that the rondo form of the interlude is itself continuing outside in the darkness. In the next scene and in the Barn Dance scene of the last act Britten's handling of intermittently-heard offstage music is much more in the well-tried tradition of Romantic opera. But here there is no offstage band. What Britten has done, in effect, is to create in his audience's minds another dimension in which an unseen but imagined space is felt to be full of unheard but imagined music. Of course there are precedents for this, too, in 19th-century opera (for example, the last act of *Rigoletto*). But this scene of *Peter Grimes* seems to me uniquely precise in its blend of realistic, formal and psychological impact. At the climax, when Grimes himself comes in to fetch his new apprentice, the formal and the psychological again move into phase with his 'Great Bear' monologue [14] introduced by a minor version (over the original 'storm' discord) of his yearning 'What harbour shelters peace' tune.

In the stretches of dialogue which, like old-fashioned recitative, carry the action forward between the more formal gestures, Britten adopts a different technique from the very strict writing of the previous two scenes. Here he uses free *secco*-type recitative over a series of tense percussion rolls. Again the balance is cleverly held between plain natural speech contours and rhythms on the one hand, and more artificial, almost sing-song, figures on the other — figures designed to tell us something more concentrated about the character. Compare Auntie's 'Him and his women' (a fine, natural contour) with her 'That is the sort of weak politeness' just afterwards, where the thought is dwelt on in a manner quite foreign to real life; or the inane canonic whining of the Nieces (not perhaps Britten's most successful creations) with Balstrode's 'D'you think we should stop our storm for such as you?' An unexpected source for this kind of writing, as for the more schematic dialogue in the first scene of the act, has been suggested* in Gershwin's *Porgy and Bess*, an idea which has the virtue of postulating a rare English-language model for lifelike conversational recitative. It seems to be confirmed, moreover, by the resemblance between the *meccanico* ostinato figure at Ellen's entrance after the 'Old Joe' round (originally the 'away from tidal waves' motif) and the crap-shooting ostinato in Act One of *Porgy*, among other similarities of detail. Britten had heard Gershwin's opera in America, and his own solitary previous stage work, *Paul Bunyan*, evidently owes still more than *Grimes* to the American show tradition.

The next three scenes all use form-building procedures in some way comparable to the one in the Boar scene, though (for reasons suggested earlier) only one of them, Act Two scene two, does it so systematically and

* Originally it seems by Bayan Northcott in a *New Statesman* review.

George Paskuda as Grimes in Wiesbaden, 1959, and Jess Thomas in San Francisco, 1973

with such power. In the other two scenes, what is involved is not much more than a relatively conventional dramatic mechanism: in the Sunday Morning scene (Act Two, scene one) the music in church provides a kind of running commentary to the developing quarrel between Ellen and Peter (in the manner of countless 19th-century operas from *Faust* to *Werther*), while the barn dance of Act Three similarly updates an ironic tradition stretching at least from *The Marriage of Figaro* to *Wozzeck*. If anything Britten outdoes his models by the pointedness of his treatment, in which irony is constantly heightened into a more specific symbolism. In the church scene the words of the Anglican matins are made to allude heavily to Grimes's troubles at almost every point: 'we have erred and strayed from thy ways' just as Ellen notices the tear in the apprentice's coat; 'O Lord open Thou our lips' with Ellen's 'John, what are you trying to hide?'; and finally 'Amen' as answer to Ellen's 'We've failed', which Peter takes up literally in his most crucial phrase 'So be it, and God have mercy upon me!' [18]. (As Philip Brett has now shown,* this was originally even more loaded, with 'He descended into Hell' answered by Peter's 'To Hell then, and God have mercy upon me'. Britten took this out, however, although he kept the obvious reference to it in Grimes's last soliloquy, 'To Hell with all your mercy'.)

*

The barn dance has, at first, only the more general ironic meaning of, for instance, the café music in *Wozzeck* (which it faintly resembles). Again the idea is taken farther: we hear a whole suite of dances, badly harmonised (perhaps!). And at the climax of the scene Britten reverts with extraordinary dramatic effect to the Ländler music of earlier on [23] — for no obvious reason, beyond the sheer Mahlerian power of the musical idea. Of all the scenes in *Peter Grimes* this is the one which most reminds one of Britten's

---

* In the Cambridge Opera Handbook.

Covent Garden, 1975: Heather Harper (Ellen) and Geraint Evans (Balstrode) with Jon Vickers (Grimes) (photo: Donald Southern)

enthusiasm for the music of the post-Romantic Viennese tradition. The links with the later scenes in *Wozzeck* are palpable. The situations of the two anti-heroes are similar: both men rejected by a hypocritical social order and about to meet an unnoticed death by water. Just as, in his murder scene, Berg heightens the tension by building his music round a single repeated note (B), so here Britten touches on the same procedure, using a held F sharp for the momentous dialogue between Ellen and Balstrode (which also partly explains the curiously inert harmonies of Ellen's song 'Embroidery in childhood'). The E flat foghorn in the mad scene is another example.

One of the 'movements' in the suite which makes up the first act of *Wozzeck* is, it may be recalled, a passacaglia, that is, a set of variations on a ground bass. It would be much too tendentious to suggest an influence on Britten in this case. Berg's use of a twelve-note theme and a 'mechanical' form parodies the pseudo-scientific obsessions of the Doctor in his dietary experiments on Wozzeck — a mere episode in the poor soldier's decline. Britten, by contrast, makes his Passacaglia the centrepiece of his drama, and uses the form to take us to the heart of Grimes's tragedy. As his mind wanders guiltily over the past and longingly towards a future which even he now realises can never be, the Passacaglia motif anchors him more and more inescapably in the present, with the posse of Borough vigilantes coming nearer and nearer. The ground-theme itself [21] is, of course, Grimes's 'God have mercy upon me' from the end of his argument with Ellen [18] (there are earlier foreshadowings of the theme, too, which need not concern us here). But in case we should be so facile as to see

26

this as a Grimes leitmotif in the Wagnerian sense explicitly rejected by Britten, we must notice the somewhat complex history of the theme *after* its first full appearance, as well as the fact that almost every theme in the opera (apart from the non-recurring tunes of some, but not all, of the individual songs) could be called a 'Grimes' leitmotif, which would leave us where we began. Certainly all the explicit references to the theme are in direct 'Grimes' contexts: where he is present or being talked about. But that is virtually the whole opera anyway. What sets this theme apart is the way Britten harps on it once it has emerged and uses it, in a number of variants, to build up the pressure on Grimes until he starts to break under the strain. From the moment that Grimes renounces salvation (in everything but his actual words) the theme pursues him as relentlessly as ever the Furies pursued Orestes. It dominates the 'Grimes is at his exercise' ensemble and chorus, and, in inversion, the ensemble which follows ('whoever's guilty gets the rap'). It gives Boles his 'She helped him in his cruel games' and the Borough its 'Speak out in the name of the Lord', one of those superb unison ejaculations which will always send shivers down the spine of anyone who hates and fears mob agreement on any subject whatever. It even invades 'We planned that their lives', which starts innocently enough. It only does not colour the beautiful 'gutter' quartet [20], where Grimes is not mentioned — a temporary release which is as happy dramatically as it is musically.

The Passacaglia Interlude (IV) itself is unusual in that the ground [21] and the variations do not coincide — there are 39 statements of the ground and ten variations, or nine if one counts the viola solo [21] as a theme (for the variations) rather than a variation (on the ground), though it is certainly that as well. In fact all the variations are dominated by the intervals of the ground, and what is astonishing, this being so, is the variety of texture and above all the freedom of rhythm Britten achieves in a form once thought rigid and constricting. The secret lies in the rhythmic and harmonic independence of the ground from the variations, and of both from the nominal 4/4 time in which the music is notated, though Britten further complicates this by making phrase-groupings of the variations irregular. It is a lucid symbol of Grimes's flailing efforts to free himself from reality.

These continue, needless to say, in the scene which follows the rise of the curtain, where Grimes's behaviour once more leads directly to the death of his apprentice. As his mind rambles from the boy to the jersey to Ellen (who knitted it), to the sea and the Borough (via the fish Grimes is going to get rich by catching), back to Ellen and the future life they will never lead because Grimes cannot escape his past — as his mind rambles in this way, so the music probes our sympathies by constant allusion back to the variations in the interlude. Some of them now take on graphic meanings which, naturally, they did not have before. The eighth variation, for instance, with its intertwining triplet quavers, now goes with Ellen embroidering, and the third variation depicts the boy weeping. Others merely maintain the general atmosphere of menace and despair, while giving shape to a scene which could otherwise so easily have become itself rambling and melodramatic. Indeed it is a feature of this scene that the tension is kept up to the very last *pizzicato*, and of course it is no accident that Britten, when he made the concert version of the fourth interlude, had to jump to the last two pages of the act to get his conclusion. Even in the opera the Passacaglia ends not when the curtain goes up but when it comes down.

Like the Boar scene, the scene in the hut includes farther-reaching reminiscence, in the big chunk of 'They listen to money' from Act One scene

Jon Vickers as Grimes at Covent Garden in 1981 (photo: Clive Barda)

one [9]. But the main role of reminiscence in *Grimes* is reserved for the final interlude and the monologue which follows it. In a sense, just as out and out dementia is less interesting than neurosis and eccentricity, so the music of these episodes, with their rather obvious distortions and wrong attributions of earlier themes, is less gripping than the Passacaglia, where Grimes was still somewhat in control of his faculties. The scene is nevertheless necessary and, if well sung and acted, very moving. One of the reasons for its effect is the astoundingly sensitive word-setting. The whole scene demonstrates admirably Britten's approach to words and his understanding of how they can be made vehicles, both for meanings which go beyond their own familiar significations, and for a special kind of music which comes, by some alchemy, from the combination of phonemes and notes. Britten himself put this well, if guardedly, when he wrote (in the 1945 Sadler's Wells Opera Book) that 'good recitative should transform the natural intonations and rhythms of everyday speech into memorable musical phrases (as with Purcell).' In fact one of the things *Peter Grimes* shows is that, for a composer of Britten's artistry, there is no clear boundary between the 'natural' speech patterns of recitative and the artificial patterns of what he called 'more stylised music'. Britten discovered early that the very act of setting words to music involves stylisation. In *Grimes* he also showed that the same is true of the act of setting drama to music.

Thematic Guide

[10] PETER
Tempo come sopra/espress.
largamente   a tempo   marcato

What har - bour shel-ters peace, a-way from ti-dal waves,

[11] *INTERLUDE II*
Presto con fuoco

ff

[12] AUNTIE
Moderato e pesante
con forza
ff

Loud man, I ne-ver did have time

[13] BALSTRODE
Allegro molto
pp

We live___ and let live,

[14] PETER
Adagio/*sostenuto*

Now_____ the Great Bear and Plei - a - des (where)

pp

pp
D.B. (+8va bassa)

[15] KEENE
Con slancio! /*leggiero*

Old Joe has gone fish-ing and Young Joe has gone fish-ing and

[16] *INTERLUDE III*
Allegro spiritoso
+8va -------------------------------

W.W.

fp   *fp*

[17] PETER
Adagio   con forza
ff ⌐3⌐   *sf*   *sf*

Take a - way your hand! Wrong to plan! Wrong to try!

[18] PETER
A tempo, energico *largamente*
ff

So be it,__ And God have mer-cy u-pon me!

[18b] AUNTIE
Allegretto
f > > >

Grimes is at his ex-er-cise!

[19] ELLEN

Larghetto/*semplice ma marcato*

We planned that their lives should have a new start,__

[20] 1st NIECE

Andante tranquillo/*marc. (senza rigore)*

From the gut-ter_____ Why should we trou – ble__

[21] *INTERLUDE IV : PASSACAGLIA*

Andante moderato/*sempre un poco rubato*   Solo Viola

pp *deliberato*   *Timp.*   *pp* *espress.*

[22] PETER

Lento tranquillo/*con espansione*

In dreams I've built my - self some kind - lier home

[23] Lento alla Ländler/*marc.*

[24] ELLEN

Andante con moto tranquillo

Em – broi – de ry in child – hood

[25] MRS SEDLEY

Him who des – pi – ses us, we'll des – troy!

31

The first foreign production of 'Grimes' was in Stockholm (1946): right: Inga Sundström & Set Svanholm. The 1948 Met. production alternated Brian Sullivan (above) & Frederick Jagel (below). Above right: Mirto Picchi (Rome, 1961). Below right: Ludmila Ravina & Petor Matves Garilkin (Moscow, 1965). Bottom: Tibor Udvardy & Maria Matyas (Budapest, 1960)

Peter Grimes

An opera in Three Acts and a Prologue
derived from the poem of George Crabbe

Words by Montagu Slater
Music by Benjamin Britten

For the Koussevitzky Music Foundation
dedicated to the memory of
Natalie Koussevitzky

Peter Grimes was first performed at Sadler's Wells, London, on June 7, 1945. It was first performed in the USA at the 1946 Berkshire Festival.

This libretto is based on the revised version published in 1961 but there were many phrases which had been altered when set to music, and the final text has been preferred here. Punctuation, spelling and the layout of ensembles have also been systematised according to what was set to music. The stage directions are, however, those in the libretto and are quite substantially different from the more extensive ones in the score.

The form of the libretto is a four-beat line with half rhythms which, according to Montagu Slater, seemed 'appropriate for the quick conversational style of the recitatives'. The prologue (apart from the chorus) is written in prose.

CHARACTERS

Peter Grimes *a fisherman*	*tenor*
Boy *his apprentice*	*silent*
Ellen Orford *a widow, schoolmistress of the Borough*	*soprano*
Captain Balstrode *retired merchant skipper*	*baritone*
Auntie *landlady of The Boar*	*contralto*
Niece 1 ⎫ *main attractions of The Boar*	*soprano*
Niece 2 ⎭	*soprano*
Robert Boles *fisherman and Methodist*	*tenor*
Swallow *a lawyer*	*bass*
Mrs (Nabob) Sedley *a rentier widow of an East India Company's factor*	*mezzo-soprano*
Rev. Horace Adams *the rector*	*tenor*
Ned Keene *apothecary and quack*	*baritone*
Dr Crabbe*	*silent*
Hobson *carrier*	*bass*

Chorus of townspeople and fisherfolk

Scene — The Borough, a small fishing town on the East Coast.

Time — Towards 1830.

---

* A late alteration: i.e. even in the vocal score, the doctor's name is given as Thorp.

Prologue

Interior of the Moot House arranged as for Coroner's Inquest. Coroner, Mr Swallow, at table on dais, clerk at table below. A crowd of townspeople in the body of the hall is kept back by Hobson acting as Constable. Mr Swallow is the leading lawyer of the Borough and at the same time its Mayor and its Coroner. A man of unexceptionable career and talents he nevertheless disturbs the burgesses by his air of a man with an arrière pensée. [1]

HOBSON
(shouts)

Peter Grimes!

Peter Grimes steps forward from among the crowd.

SWALLOW

Peter Grimes, we are here to investigate the cause of death of your apprentice William Spode, whose body you brought ashore from your boat, 'The Boy Billy', on the 26th, ultimo. Do you wish to give evidence?
(Peter nods.)
Will you step into the box? Peter Grimes. Take the oath. After me. 'I swear by Almighty God.'

PETER

'I swear by Almighty God.'

SWALLOW

'That the evidence I shall give.'

PETER

'That the evidence I shall give.'

SWALLOW

'Shall be the truth.'

PETER

'Shall be the truth.'

SWALLOW

'The whole truth and nothing but the truth!'

PETER

'The whole truth and nothing but the truth!'

SWALLOW

Tell the court the story in your own words.
(Peter is silent.)
You sailed your boat round the coast with the intention of putting in at London. Why did you do this?

PETER

We'd caught a huge catch, too big to sell here.

SWALLOW

And the boy died on the way?

PETER

The wind turned against us, blew us off our course. We ran out of drinking water.

SWALLOW

How long were you at sea?

PETER

Three days.
[2]

SWALLOW

What happened next?

PETER

He died lying there among the fish.

SWALLOW

What did you do?

PETER

Threw them all overboard, set sail for home.

SWALLOW

You mean you threw the fish overboard? When you landed did you call for help?

PETER

I called Ned Keene.

SWALLOW

The apothecary here?
(indicates Ned)
Was there anybody else called?

PETER

Somebody brought the parson.

SWALLOW

You mean the rector, Mr Horace Adams?
(The Rector steps forward. Swallow waves him back.)
All right Mr Adams.
(He turns back to Peter.)
Was there a certain amount of excitement?

PETER

Bob Boles started shouting.

SWALLOW

There was a scene in the village street from which you were rescued by our landlady?

PETER

Yes. By Auntie.

SWALLOW

We don't call her that here! . . . You then took to abusing a respectable lady?

Peter glares.

SWALLOW

Answer me . . . You shouted abuse at a certain person?

Mrs Sedley pushes forward. Mrs Sedley is the widow of a retired factor of the East India Company and is known locally as 'Mrs Nabob'. She is 65, self-assertive, inquisitive, unpopular.

MRS SEDLEY

Say who! Say who!!

SWALLOW

Mrs Sedley here.

PETER
(fiercely)

I don't like interferers.

A slight hubbub among the spectators resolves itself into a chorus which is more like the confused muttering of a crowd than something fully articulate.

CHORUS

When women gossip the result
Is, someone doesn't sleep at night!

HOBSON
(shouting)

Silence!

SWALLOW

Now tell me this. Who helped you carry the boy home? The schoolmistress, the widow, Mrs Ellen Orford?

WOMEN'S CHORUS

Oh when you pray, you shut your eyes,
You then can't tell the truth from lies!

HOBSON
(shouts)

Silence!

SWALLOW

Mrs Orford, as the schoolmistress, the widow, how did you come into this?

ELLEN

I did what I could to help.

SWALLOW

Why should you help this kind of fellow—
callous, brutal, coarse?
(to Grimes)
There's something here perhaps in your

favour. I am told you rescued this boy from drowning in the March storms.
(Peter is silent.)
Have you something else to say?
No?—Then I have.
(Swallow rises.)
Peter Grimes, I here advise you—do not get another boy apprentice. Get a fisherman to help you—big enough to stand up for himself. Our verdict is—that William Spode, your apprentice, died in accidental circumstances. But that's the kind of thing people are apt to remember.

CHORUS

But when the crowner sits upon it,
Who can dare to fix the guilt?

HOBSON
(shouts)

Silence! Silence!

Peter has stepped forward and is trying to speak.

PETER

Your honour! Like every other fisherman I have to hire an apprentice. I must have help—

SWALLOW

Then get a woman help you look after him.

PETER

That's what I want—but not yet—

SWALLOW

Why not?

PETER

Not till I've stopped people's mouths.

The hubbub begins again.

SWALLOW
(makes a gesture of dismissal)

Stand down! Clear the court. Stand down!

PETER

'Stand down', you say. You wash your
hands.
The case goes on in people's minds.
The charges that no court has made
Will be shouted at my head.
Then let me speak, let me stand trial,
Bring the accusers into the hall.
Let me thrust into their mouths
The truth itself, the simple truth.

He shouts this excitedly against the hubbub chorus.

CHORUS

When women gossip the result
Is, someone doesn't sleep at night.
But when the crowner sits upon it,
Who can dare to fix the guilt?

(Against them all Constable Hobson shouts his:)

HOBSON

Clear the court!

Swallow rises with slow dignity. Everybody stands up while he makes his ceremonial exit. The crowd then begins to go out. Peter and Ellen are left alone.

PETER

The truth—the pity—and the truth.

ELLEN

Peter, come away!

PETER

Where the walls themselves
Gossip of inquest.

ELLEN

But we'll gossip, too,
And talk and rest.

PETER

While Peeping Toms
Nod as you go.
You'll share the name
Of outlaw, too!

ELLEN

Peter, we shall restore your name.
Warmed by the new esteem
That you will find.

PETER

Until the Borough hate
Poisons your mind.

ELLEN

There'll be new shoals to catch,
Life will be kind.

PETER

Ay! Only of drowning ghosts:
Time will not forget,
The dead are witness,
And fate is blind.

ELLEN

Unclouded,
The hot sun
Will spread his rays around.

ELLEN AND PETER

My ⎫
Your ⎭ voice out of the pain,
Is like a hand
That { you / I } can feel and know:
Here is a friend.

They walk off slowly as the curtain falls.

Interlude I [3]

The Prologue in the production by Colin Graham for Opera North with Ava June (Ellen), Robert Ferguson (Grimes) and Harold Blackburn (Swallow) (photo: Terry Cryer)

Act One

Scene One. *Street by the sea; Moot Hall exterior with its outside staircase, next door to which is The Boar. Ned Keene's apothecary's shop is at the street corner. On the other side breakwaters run down to the sea.*

It is morning, before high tide, several days later.

Two fishermen are turning the capstan, hauling in their boat. Prolonged cries as the boat is hauled ashore. Women come from mending nets to take the fish baskets from other fishermen who now disembark.

Captain Balstrode sits on the breakwater looking out to sea through his glass. Balstrode is a retired merchant sea-captain, shrewd as a travelled man should be, but with a general sympathy that makes him the favourite rentier of the whole Borough. He chews a plug of tobacco while he watches.

Chorus of fishermen and women.

CHORUS [4]

Oh, hang at open doors the net, the cork,
While squalid sea-dames at their mending
   work.
Welcome the hour when fishing through
   the tide
The weary husband throws his freight aside.

FISHERMEN

Oh, cold and wet, and driven by the tide,
Beat your tired arms against your tarry side.
Find rest in public bars where fiery gin
Will aid the warmth that languishes within.

Several fishermen cross to The Boar where Auntie stands in the doorway.

FISHERMAN

Auntie!

AUNTIE

Come in gentlemen, come in.

BOLES

Her vats flow with poisoned gin.

Boles, the Methodist fisherman, stands aside from all this dram drinking.

FISHERMAN
(points and laughs)

Boles has gone Methody.

AUNTIE

A man should have
Hobbies to cheer his private life!

Fishermen go into The Boar. Others remain with their wives at the nets and boats.

CHORUS OF WOMEN

Dabbling on shore half-naked sea-boys
   crowd,
Swim round a ship, or swing upon a
   shroud:
Or in a boat purloined with paddles play
And grow familiar with the watery way.

While the second boat is being hauled in, boys are scrambling over the first.

BALSTRODE

Shoo you little barnacles!
Up your anchors! Hoist your sails!

Balstrode chases them from the boat. A more respectable figure now begins, with much hat-raising, his morning progress down the High Street. He makes straight for The Boar.

FISHERMAN
(touches cap)

Dr Crabbe.

BOLES
(points as the swing door closes)

He drinks 'Good Health' to all diseases.

FISHERMAN

Storm?

OTHER FISHERMEN

Storm?

They shade their eyes looking out to sea.

BALSTRODE
(glass to his eye)

A long way out. Sea horses.
The wind is holding back the tide.
If it veers round, watch for your lives.

CHORUS

And if the springtide eats the land again,
Till even the cottages and cobbled walls of
   fishermen
Are billets for the thieving waves which
   take
As if in sleep, thieving for thieving's sake.

*The Rector comes down the High Street.
He is followed as always by the Borough's
second most famous rentier, the widow,
Mrs (Nabob) Sedley. From The Boar
come the two 'nieces' who give Auntie her
nickname. They stand in front of the pub
taking the morning sun. Ned Keene, seeing
Mrs Sedley, pops out of his shop door.*

RECTOR
(*right and left*)

Good morning, good morning!

NIECES

Good morning!

MRS SEDLEY

Good morning, dear Rector.

NED

Had Auntie no nieces we'd never respect
her!

SWALLOW

Good morning, good morning!

NIECES

Good morning!

MRS SEDLEY

Good morning, your worship, Mr Swallow!

AUNTIE
(*to Keene*)

You jeer, but if they wink you're eager to
follow.

*The Rector and Mrs Sedley continue
towards the church.*

NED
(*shouts across to Auntie*)

I'm coming tonight to see your nieces!

AUNTIE
(*dignified*)

'The Boar' is at its patrons' service.

BOLES

God's storm will drown your hot desires!

BALSTRODE

God stay the tide, or I shall share your
fears.

CHORUS

For us sea-dwellers this sea-birth can be
Death to our gardens of fertility.
Yet only such contemptuous springtide
can
Tickle the virile impotence of man.

PETER
(*calls off*)

Hi! Give us a hand!

(*Chorus stops.*)
Haul the boat!

BOLES
(*shouts back*)

Haul it yourself, Grimes!

PETER
(*off*)

Hi! Somebody bring the rope!

*Nobody does. Presently he appears and takes
the capstan rope himself and pulls it after
him (off) to the boat. Then he returns. The
fishermen and women turn their backs on
him and slouch away awkwardly. Balstrode
and Keene move to the capstan.*

BALSTRODE [5]
(*going to capstan*)

I'll give a hand. The tide is near the turn.

NED

We'll drown the gossips in a tidal storm.

*Grimes goes back to the boat. Balstrode
and Keene turn capstan.*

AUNTIE
(*at the door of The Boar*)

Parsons may moralise and fools decide,
But a good publican takes neither side.

BALSTRODE

Oh haul away, the tide is near the turn.

NED

Man invented morals but tides have none.

BOLES
(*with arms akimbo watches their labour*)

This lost soul of a fisherman must be
Shunned by respectable society!
Oh let the captains hear, let the scholars
learn:
Shielding the sin, they share the people's
scorn.

AUNTIE

I have my business. Let the preachers learn,
Hell may be fiery but the pub won't burn.

BALSTRODE AND NED

The tide that floods will ebb, the tide will
turn!

The boat is hauled up. Grimes appears.

NED

Grimes, you won't need help from now.
I've got a prentice for you.

BALSTRODE

A workhouse brat?

NED

I called at the workhouse yesterday.
All you do now is fetch the boy.

We'll send the carter with a note.
He'll bring your bargain on his cart!
(*shouts*)
Jim Hobson, we've a job for you.

HOBSON
(*enters*)

Cart's full, sir. More than I can do.

NED

Listen, Jim. You'll go to the workhouse
And ask for Mr Keene his purchase.
Bring him back to Grimes!

HOBSON

Cart's full, sir, I have no room.

NED

Hobson, you'll do what there is to be done.

*It is near enough to an argument to attract
a crowd. Fishermen and women gather round.
Boles takes his chance.*

BOLES

Is this a Christian country? Are
Pauper children so enslaved
That their bodies go for cash?

NED

Hobson, will you do your job?

*Ellen Orford has come in. She is a widow
of about 40. Her children have died, or
grown up and gone away, and in her
loneliness she has become the Borough
schoolmistress. A hard life has not hardened
her. It has made her the more charitable.*

HOBSON [6]

I have to go from pub to pub,
Picking up parcels, standing about.
My journey back is late at night.
Mister, find some other way
To bring your boy back.

CHORUS

He's right. Dirty jobs!

HOBSON

Mister, find some other . . .

ELLEN

Carter! I'll mind your passenger.

CHORUS

What? And be Grimes's messenger?

ELLEN

Whatever you say, I'm not ashamed.
Somebody must do the job.
The carter goes from pub to pub,
Picking up parcels, standing about.
The boy needs comfort late at night.
He needs a welcome on the road,
Coming here strange he'll be afraid.
I'll mind your passenger!

NED

Mrs Orford is talking sense—

CHORUS

Ellen—you're leading us a dance,
Fetching boys for Peter Grimes,
Because the Boro' is afraid,
You who help will share the blame!

ELLEN

Whatever you say . . .
Let her among you without fault
Cast the first stone
And let the Pharisees and Saducees
Give way to none.
But whosoever feels his pride
Humbled so deep,
There is no corner he can hide
Even in sleep,
Will have no trouble to find out
How a poor teacher,
Widowed and lonely, finds delight
In shouldering care.
(*as she moves up the street*)
Mr Hobson, where's your cart?
I'm ready.

HOBSON

Up here, ma'am. I can wait.

*The crowd stands round and watches.
Some follow Ellen and Hobson. On the
edge of the crowd are other activities.*

MRS SEDLEY
(*whispers to Ned*)

Have you my pills?

NED

I'm sorry, ma'am.

MRS SEDLEY

My sleeping draught?

NED

The laudanum
Is out of stock, and being brought
By Mr Carrier Hobson's car.
He's back tonight.

MRS SEDLEY

Good lord, good lord—

NED

Meet us both in the pub, The Boar,
Auntie's we call it. It's quite safe.

MRS SEDLEY

I've never been in a pub in my life.

NED

You'll come?

MRS SEDLEY

All right!

NED

Tonight?

MRS SEDLEY

All right!

She moves off up the street.

NED

If the old dear takes much more laudanum,
She'll land herself one day in Bedlam!

BALSTRODE

(looks seaward through his glass)

Look! The storm cone!
The wind veers
In from the sea
At gale force!

CHORUS

Look out for squalls.
It's veering in from sea!
The wind veers
In at gale force.

Make your boat fast!
Shutter your windows!
And bring in all the nets!

ALL [7]

Now the flood tide
And sea-horses
Will gallop over
The eroded coast!

The wind veers
In from sea
At gale force.
Flooding, flooding
Our seasonal fears.
Look! The storm cone!

As the wind veers,
A high tide coming
Will eat the land.
A tide no breakwaters can withstand.
Fasten your boats. The springtide's here
With a gale behind.

CHORUS

Is there much to fear?

NED

Only for the goods you're rich in!
It won't drown your conscience, it might
flood your kitchen.

BOLES

(passionately)

God has his ways which are not ours,
His high tide swallows up the shores.
Repent!

NED

And keep your wife upstairs!

OMNES

O Tide that waits for no man,
Spare our coast!

*There is a General Exeunt—mostly
through the swing doors of The Boar. Dr
Crabbe's hat blows away, is rescued for
him by Ned Keene who bows him into the
pub. Finally only Peter and Balstrode are
left, Peter gazing seaward, Balstrode hesi-
tating at the pub door.*

BALSTRODE

And do you prefer the storm
To Auntie's parlour and the rum?

PETER

I live alone. The habit grows.

BALSTRODE

Grimes, since you're a lonely soul,
Born to blocks and spars and ropes,
Why not try the wider sea
With merchantman or privateer?

PETER

I am native, rooted here.

BALSTRODE

Rooted by what?

PETER

By familiar fields,
Marsh and sand,
Ordinary streets,
Prevailing wind.

BALSTRODE

You'd slip these moorings, if you had the
mind.

PETER

By the shut faces
Of the Borough clans,
And by the kindness
Of a casual glance.

BALSTRODE

You'll find no comfort there.

When an urchin's quarrelsome,
Brawling at his little games,
Mother stops him with the threat—
'You'll be sold to Peter Grimes.'

PETER

Selling me new apprentices,
Children taught to be ashamed
Of the legend on their faces—
'You've been sold to Peter Grimes!'

BALSTRODE

Then the Crowner sits to
Hint, but not to mention crimes,
And publishes an open verdict
Whispered about this 'Peter Grimes'.

Your boy was workhouse starved—
Maybe you're not to blame he died.

PETER [8]

Picture what that day was like,
That evil day!
We strained into the wind,
Heavily laden.
Plunged into the waves'
Shuddering challenge.
Then the sea rose to a storm
Over the gunwales,
And the child's silent reproach
Turned to illness.
Then home
Among fishing nets,
Alone, alone, alone
With a childish death.

BALSTRODE

This storm is useful. You can speak your
   mind
And never mind the Borough commentary.
There is more grandeur in a gale of wind
To free confession, set a conscience free.

PETER [9]

They listen to money
These Borough gossips;
I have my visions,
Fiery visions.
They call me dreamer,
They scoff at my dreams
And my ambition.
But I know a way
To answer the Borough;
I'll win them over.

BALSTRODE

With the new prentice?

PETER

We'll sail together.
These Borough gossips
Listen to money,
Only to money:
I'll fish the sea dry,
Sell the good catches—
That wealthy merchant
Grimes will set up
Household and shop,
You will all see it!
I'll marry Ellen.

BALSTRODE

Man—go and ask her,
Without your booty,
She'll have you now.

PETER

No—not for pity! . . .

BALSTRODE

Then the old tragedy
Is in store:

New start with new prentice
Just as before!

PETER

What Peter Grimes decides
Is his affair!

BALSTRODE

      You fool, man, you fool!

*The wind has risen, Balstrode is shouting
above it. Peter faces him angrily.*

PETER

Are you my conscience?

BALSTRODE

         Might as well
Try shout the wind down as to tell
The obvious truth!

PETER

        Take your advice—
Put it where your money is!

BALSTRODE

The storm is here. Oh, come away.

PETER

The storm is here and I shall stay.

*The storm is rising. Auntie comes out of
'The Boar' to fasten the shutters, in front of
the windows. Balstrode goes to help her.
He looks back towards Peter, then goes
into the pub.*

What harbour shelters peace?   [10]
Away from tidal waves, away from storms,
What harbour can embrace
Terrors and tragedies?
With her there'll be no quarrels,
With her the mood will stay,
Her breast is harbour too,
Where night is turned to day.

*The wind rises. He stands a moment as if
leaning against the wind.*

Curtain.

Interlude II [11]

Scene Two. *Interior of The Boar, typical
main room of a country pub. No bar.
Upright settles, tables, log fire. When the
curtain rises Auntie is admitting Mrs Sedley.
The gale has risen to hurricane force and
Auntie holds the door with difficulty against
the wind which rattles the windows and
howls in the chimney. They both push the
door closed.*

AUNTIE

Past time to close!

MRS SEDLEY

      He said half-past ten.

AUNTIE

Who?

MRS SEDLEY

Mr Keene.

AUNTIE

Him and his women!

MRS SEDLEY

You referring to me?

AUNTIE

Not at all, not at all!
What do you want?

MRS SEDLEY

Room from the storm.

AUNTIE

That is the sort of weak politeness
Makes a publican lose her clients.
Keep in the corner out of sight!

*Balstrode and a fisherman enter. They
struggle with the door.*

BALSTRODE

Phew, that's a bitch of a gale all right.

AUNTIE
(*nods her head towards Mrs Sedley*)

Sh-h-h.

BALSTRODE

Sorry. I didn't see you, missis.
You'll give the regulars a surprise.

AUNTIE

She's meeting Ned.

BALSTRODE

Which Ned?

AUNTIE

The quack!
He's looking after her heart attack.

BALSTRODE

Bring us a pint.

AUNTIE

It's closing time.

BALSTRODE

You fearful old female—why should *you*
mind?

AUNTIE

The storm!

*Bob Boles and other fishermen enter. The
wind howls through the door and again
there is difficulty in closing it.*

BOLES

Did you hear the tide
Has broken over the Northern Road?

*He leaves the door open too long with
disastrous consequences. A sudden gust
howls through the door, the shutters of the
window fly open, a pane blows in.*

BALSTRODE
(*shouts*)

Get those shutters.

AUNTIE
(*screams*)

O-o-o-o-o!

BALSTRODE

You fearful old female, why do you
Leave your windows naked?

AUNTIE

O-o-o-o-o!

BALSTRODE

Better strip a niece or two
And clamp your shutters!

*The two 'nieces' run in. They are young,
pretty enough though a little worn, conscious
that they are the chief attraction of The
Boar. At the moment they are in mild
hysterics, having run downstairs in their
night clothes, though with their unusual
instinct for precaution they have found time
to don each a wrap. It is not clear whether
they are sisters, friends or simply colleagues:
but they behave like twins, as though each
has only half a personality and they cling
together always to sustain their self-esteem.*

NIECES

Oo! Oo!
It's blown our bedroom windows in.
Oo! We'll all be drowned.

BALSTRODE

Perhaps in gin!

NIECES

I wouldn't mind if it didn't howl.
It gets on my nerves.
We'll all be drowned.
I wouldn't mind if it didn't howl.

BALSTRODE

D'you think we
Should stop our storm for such as you –
Coming all over palpitations!
Auntie, get some new relations!

AUNTIE [12]
(*takes it ill*)

Loud man, I never did have time
For the kind of creature who spits in his
wine!

43

A joke's a joke and fun is fun
But say your grace and be polite for all that
  we have done.

NIECES

For his peace of mind.

MRS SEDLEY

This is no place for me.

AUNTIE

Loud man, you're glad enough to be
Playing your cards in our company.
A joke's a joke and fun is fun
But say your grace and be polite for all that
  we have done.

NIECES

For his peace of mind.

MRS SEDLEY

This is no place for me.

AUNTIE

Loud man –!

*Two fishermen enter. Usual struggle with
the door.*

FIRST FISHERMAN

There's been a landslide up the coast!

BOLES
(*rising unsteadily*)

I'm drunk! Drunk!

BALSTRODE

You're a Methody wastrel!

BOLES
(*staggers to one of the nieces*)

Is this a niece of yours?

AUNTIE

     That's so.

BOLES

Who's her father?

AUNTIE

     Who wants to know?

BOLES

I want to pay my best respects
To the beauty and misery of her sex.

BALSTRODE

Old Methody, you'd better tune
Your piety to another hymn!

BOLES

I want her!

BALSTRODE

Sh-h-h!

AUNTIE
(*cold*)

Turn that man out.

BALSTRODE

Auntie, he's the local preacher.
He's lost the way of carrying liquor.
He means no harm.

BOLES

No, I mean love!

BALSTRODE

     Come on, boy!

*Boles hits him. Mrs Sedley screams.
Balstrode quietly overpowers Boles and sits
him in a chair.*

We live and let live, and look,   [13]
We keep our hands to ourselves.

*Boles struggles to his feet, Balstrode sits him
down again, laying the law down.*

Pub conversation should depend
On this eternal moral;
So long as satire don't descend
To fisticuff or quarrel.
We live and let live, and look,
We keep our hands to ourselves.

*And while Boles is being forced into his chair
again the bystanders comment:*

CHORUS

We live and let live, and look,
We keep our hands to ourselves!

BALSTRODE

We sit and drink the evening through
Not deigning to devote a
Thought to the daily cud we chew
But buying drinks by rota!
We live and let live, and look,
We keep our hands to ourselves.

    And chorus as before.

*The door opens. The struggle with the wind
is worse than before as Ned Keene gets
through.*

NED

Have you heard? The cliff is down
Up by Grimes's hut.

AUNTIE

     Where is he?

MRS SEDLEY

Thank God you've come!

NED

     You won't blow away.

MRS SEDLEY

The carter's over half an hour late!

BALSTRODE

He'll be later still: the road's under flood.

MRS SEDLEY

I can't stay longer – I refuse!

NED

You'll have to stay if you want your pills.

MRS SEDLEY

With drunken females and in brawls!

NED

They're Auntie's nieces, that's what they
    are,
And better than you for kissing, ma!
Mind that door!

ALL

Mind that door!

*The door opens again. Peter Grimes has
come in. Unlike the rest he wears no oilskins.
His hair looks wild. He advances into the
room shaking off the raindrops from his
hair. Mrs Sedley faints. Ned Keene catches
her as she falls.*

NED

Get the brandy, Aunt.

AUNTIE

                        Who'll pay?

NED

Her! I'll charge her for it.

CHORUS

Talk of the devil and there he is.
And a devil he *is*! And a devil he *is*!
Grimes is waiting his apprentice.

*Peter sits down. The others move away from
that side of the table.*

NED

This widow's as strong as any two
Fishermen I have met.
Everybody's very quiet!

*No-one answers. Silence is broken by Peter,
as if thinking aloud.*

PETER [14]

Now the Great Bear and Pleiades
    where earth moves
Are drawing up the clouds
    of human grief
Breathing solemnity in the deep night.

Who can decipher
    in storm or starlight
The written character
    of a friendly fate –
As the sky turns, the world for us to change?

But if the horoscope's
    bewildering,
Like flashing turmoil
    of a shoal of herring,
Who can turn skies back and begin again?

Silence again. Then muttering in undertones.

CHORUS

He's mad or drunk.
                        Why's that man here?

NIECES

His song alone would sour the beer.

CHORUS

His temper's up.
                        Oh chuck him out!

NIECES

I wouldn't mind if he didn't howl!

CHORUS

He looks as if he's nearly drowned.

BOLES
(*He staggers up to Grimes.*)

You've sold your soul, Grimes!

BALSTRODE

Come away.

BOLES

            Satan's got no hold on me.

BALSTRODE

Leave him alone, you drunkard!

    He goes to get hold of Boles.

BOLES

I'll hold the gospel light before
The cataract that blinds his eyes.

PETER
(*as the drunk stumbles up to him*)

Get out.

*Grimes thrusts Boles aside roughly and
turns away.*

BOLES

        His exercise
Is not with men but killing boys.

*Boles picks up a bottle and is about to bring
it down on Grimes's head when Balstrode
knocks it out of his hand and it crashes in
fragments on the floor.*

AUNTIE

For God's sake, help me keep the peace.
D'you want me up at the next Assize?

BALSTRODE

For peace sake, someone start a song.

ALL [15]
(*led by Ned and then Auntie*)

Old Joe has gone fishing and
Young Joe has gone fishing and
You Know has gone fishing and
Found them a shoal.
Pull them in in han'fuls,
And in canfuls,
And in panfuls.
Bring them in sweetly,
Gut them completely,
Pack them up neatly.
Sell them discreetly.
Oh, haul a-way!

Peter comes into the round; the course of the round is upset.

PETER

When I had gone fishing,
When he had gone fishing,
When You Know'd gone fishing,
We found us Davy Jones.
Bring him in with horror!
Bring him in with terror!
And bring him in with sorrow!
Oh, haul a-way!

This breaks the round, but the others recover in a repeat.

At the climax of the round the door opens to admit Ellen Orford, the boy and the carrier. All three are soaking, muddy and bedraggled.

HOBSON

The bridge is down, we half swam over.

NED

And your cart? Is it seaworthy?

The women go to Ellen and the boy. Auntie fusses over them. Boles reproaches.

ELLEN

We're chilled to the bone.

BOLES
(*to Ellen*)

Serves you right, woman.

AUNTIE

My dear,
There's brandy and hot water to spare.

NIECES

Let's look at the boy.

ELLEN
(*rising*)

Let him be.

NIECES
(*admiring*)

Nice sweet thing.

ELLEN
(*protecting him*)

Not for such as you.

PETER

Let's go. You ready?

AUNTIE

Let them warm up.
They've been half drowned.

PETER

Time to get off!

AUNTIE

Your hut's washed away.

PETER

Only the cliff.
Young prentice, come!

The boy hesitates, Ellen leads him to Peter.

ELLEN

Goodbye, my dear, God bless you.
Peter will take you home.

OMNES
(*except Peter and Ellen*)

Home? Do you call that home?

Peter takes the boy out of the door into the storm.

Curtain.

Act Two

Scene One. *Scene as in Act One. The Street. A fine sunny morning, some weeks later.*

The street is deserted till Ellen and the boy, John, enter. Ellen is carrying a work-basket. She sits down between a boat and a break-water and takes her knitting from the basket. One or two late-comers cross and hurry into the church.

ELLEN

Glitter of waves
And glitter of sunlight
Bid us rejoice
And lift our hearts on high.

Man alone
Has a soul to save,
And goes to church
To worship on a Sunday.

(*The organ starts a voluntary in church.*)

Shall we not go to church this Sunday,
But do our knitting by the sea?
I'll do the work. You talk.

Hymn starts in church.

CONGREGATION

Now that the daylight fills the sky,
We lift our hearts to God on high,
That He in all we do or say
Would keep us free from harm to-day.

ELLEN

Nothing to tell me,
Nothing to say? Then shall I
Tell you what your life was like?
See if I'm right. I think
You liked your workhouse with its grave
Empty look. Perhaps you weren't
So unhappy in your loneliness?

When first I started teaching,
The life at school seemed bleak and empty,
But soon I found a way of knowing
  children –
Found the woes of little people
Hurt more, but are more simple.

She goes on with her work. John says nothing.

CONGREGATION

May he restrain our tongues from strife,
Shield from anger's din our life,
And guard with watchful care our eyes
From earth's absorbing vanities!

ELLEN

John, you may have heard the stories
Of the prentice Peter had before:

CONGREGATION

So we, when this day's work is done
And shades of night return once more.
  Amen.

ELLEN

But when you came, I
Said: now this is where we
Make a new start. Every day
I pray it may be so.

Morning prayer begins. The Rector's voice is heard.

RECTOR

Wherefore, I pray and beseech you, as many as are here present, to accompany me with a pure heart and humble voice, saying after me . . .

CONGREGATION

Almighty and most merciful Father, we have erred and strayed from Thy ways like lost sheep . . .

The prayer continues through the ensuing scene.

ELLEN

There's a tear in your coat. Was that done
Before you came?
          Badly torn.
That was done recently.
Take your hand away.
Your neck is it? John, what
Are you trying to hide?

RECTOR
(*in church*)

O Lord open Thou our lips!

CHOIR

And our mouth shall show forth Thy praise.

RECTOR

O God make speed to save us!

CHOIR

O Lord make haste to help us.

Ellen undoes the neck of the shirt.

ELLEN

A bruise.
      Well . . . It's begun.

RECTOR

Glory be to the Father and to the Son . . .

CHOIR

And to the Holy Ghost.

RECTOR

As it was in the beginning, is now . . .

ELLEN

Child you're not too young to know
Where roots of sorrow are.
Innocent, you've learned how near
Life is to torture!

RECTOR

Praise ye the Lord!

CHOIR

The Lord's name be praised.

ELLEN

Let this be a holiday,
Full of peace and quietness,
While the treason of the waves
Glitters like love.

Storm and all its terrors are
Nothing to the heart's despair.
After the storm will come a sleep,
Like oceans deep!

CHOIR
(*off*)

O all ye Works of the Lord, bless ye the
    Lord;
O ye Sun and Moon, bless ye the Lord;
O ye Winds of God, bless ye the Lord,
Praise Him and magnify Him for ever.

Peter Grimes enters.

O ye Light and Darkness, bless ye the Lord;
O ye Nights and Days, bless ye the Lord;
O ye Lightnings and Clouds, bless ye the
    Lord;
Praise Him and magnify Him for ever.

PETER

Come boy.

ELLEN

Peter — what for?

CHOIR
(*off*)

O ye Wells, bless ye the Lord;
O ye Seas and Floods, bless ye the Lord;
O ye Whales and all that move in the waters;
Praise Him and magnify Him for ever.

PETER

I've seen a shoal, I need his help.

ELLEN

But if there were, then all the boats
Would fast be launching.

PETER

I can see
The shoals to which the rest are blind.

CHOIR
(*off*)

O all ye Fowls of the air, bless ye the Lord;
O all ye Beasts and Cattle, bless ye the Lord;
O all ye Children of Men, bless ye the Lord;
Praise him and magnify Him for ever.

ELLEN

This is a Sunday, his day of rest.

PETER

This is whatever day I say it is!
Come boy!

ELLEN

You and John have fished all week –
Night and day without a break –
Painting boat and mending nets,
Now let him rest.

PETER

Come boy!

ELLEN

But your bargain . . .

PETER

My bargain?

ELLEN

His weekly rest.

PETER

He works for me, leave him alone, he's mine!

ELLEN

Hush, Peter!

CHOIR
(*off*)

O ye Servants of the Lord, bless ye the Lord;
O ye holy and humble, bless ye the Lord,
Ananias, Azarias and Misael, bless ye the
    Lord;
Praise Him and magnify Him for ever.
Glory be to the Father and to the Son, and
    to the Holy Ghost,
As it was in the beginning is now and ever
    shall be,
World without end. Amen.

*The sound dies down. In church the lesson is
being read.*

ELLEN

This unrelenting work,
This grey, unresting industry –
What aim, what future,
What peace will your hard profits buy?

PETER

Buy us a home, buy us respect,

48

And buy us freedom from pain
Of grinning at gossips' tales.
Believe in me, we shall be free!

CHOIR
(off)

I believe in God the Father Almighty,
Maker of Heaven and earth:
And in Jesus Christ his only son . . .

(fades into the background)

ELLEN

Peter, tell me one thing, where
The youngster got that ugly bruise?

PETER

Out of the hurly burly.

ELLEN

          Oh, your ways
Are hard and rough beyond his days.
Peter, were we right in what we planned
To do? Were we right? Were we right?

PETER

Take away your hand!   [17]
(then quietly)
My only hope depends on you.
If you – take it away – what's left?

ELLEN

Were we mistaken when we schemed
To solve your life by lonely toil?

PETER
(in anger)

Wrong to plan?   [17]
Wrong to try?
Wrong to live?
Right to die?

ELLEN

Were we mistaken when we dreamed
That we'd come through and all be well?

PETER

Wrong to struggle?
Wrong to hope?
Then the Borough's
Right again?

ELLEN

Peter! You cannot buy your peace
You'll never stop the gossips' talk,
With all the fish from out the sea.
We were mistaken to have dreamed . . .
Peter! We've failed! We've failed!

*He cries out as if in agony, then strikes her.
The basket falls.*

PETER [18a]

So be it! – And God have mercy upon me!

*The boy runs from him. Peter follows. Ellen
watches, then goes out the other way. Behind
closed doors and half-open windows neighbours have been watching. Three now emerge.
First Auntie, then Ned Keene, finally Boles.*

AUNTIE

Fool! To let it come to this!
Wasting pity, squandering tears.
Grimes is at his exercise.   [18b]

NED

See the glitter in his eyes!
Grimes is at his exercise.

BOLES

What he fears is that the Lord
Follows with a flaming sword!

AUNTIE

You see all thro' crazy eyes.

ALL THREE

Grimes is at his exercise.

BOLES

Where's the pastor of this flock?
Where the guardian shepherd's hook?

ALL THREE

Parson, lawyer, all at prayers.

*In church, the Benediction. Then the con-
gregation emerges.*

Now the church parade begins.
Fresh beginning for fresh sins.
Ogling with a pious gaze,
Each one's at his exercise.

Doctor Crabbe comes first.

AUNTIE

Doctor!

NED

Leave him out of it!

MRS SEDLEY
(from church)

What is it?

NED

Private business!

MRS SEDLEY

I heard two voices during psalms,
One was Grimes, and one more calm.

BOLES
(to a fisherwoman as she comes out)

While you worshipped idols there
The Devil had his Sabbath here.

MRS SEDLEY

Maltreating that poor boy again!

BALSTRODE

Grimes is weatherwise and skilled
In the practice of his trade.
Let him be. Let us forget
What slander can invent!

CHORUS

What is it?

AUNTIE, BOLES AND NED

What do you suppose?
Grimes is at his exercise.

CHORUS

What is it? What do you suppose?
Grimes is at his exercise.

*As people come out two by two they circulate
the village green singing their couplets as
they reach the centre. First come Swallow
and a fellow lawyer.*

FELLOW LAWYER

Dullards build their self-esteem
By inventing cruelties.

SWALLOW

Even so, the law restrains
Too impetuous enterprise.

A FISHERWOMAN

Fishing is a lonely trade,
Single men have much to bear.

NIECES

If a man's work cannot be made
Decent, let him stay ashore.

CHORUS
(*over all*)

What is it? What do you suppose?
Grimes is at his exercise.

RECTOR

My flock – ah, what a weight is this,
My burden pastoral.

MRS SEDLEY

But what a dangerous faith is this
That gives souls equality!

Balstrode pauses by Ned as he walks round.

BALSTRODE

When the Borough gossip starts
Somebody will suffer!

CHORUS

What is it? What do you suppose?
Grimes is at his exercise.

*During the hubbub Boles climbs a little way
up the steps of the Moot Hall.*

BOLES

People – . . . No! I will speak!
This thing here concerns you all.

CHORUS
(*crowding round Boles*)

Whoever's guilty gets the rap!
The Borough keeps its standards up.

BALSTRODE

Tub-thumping.

BOLES

This prentice system's
Uncivilised, and unchristian.

BALSTRODE

Something of the sort befits
Brats conceived outside the sheets.

BOLES

Where's the parson in his black?
Is he here or is he not?
To guide a sinful, straying flock?

CHORUS

Where's the parson?

RECTOR

Is it my business?

BOLES

Your business? To ignore,
Growing at your door,
Evils, like your fancy flowers?

CHORUS

Evils!

RECTOR

Calm now, tell me what it is.

*Ellen comes in. She is met by Auntie who
has picked up Ellen's abandoned basket and
its contents.*

AUNTIE

Ellen dear, see I've gathered
All your things. Come, rest inside!

BOLES AND CHORUS

She can tell you, Ellen Orford.
She helped him in his cruel games!

RECTOR
(*holding his hand up for silence*)

Ellen, please!

ELLEN

What am I to do?

BOLES AND CHORUS

Speak out in the name of the Lord!

ELLEN [19]

We planned that their lives should
Have a new start,
That I as a friend could
Make the plan work,
By bringing comfort where
Their lives were stark.

RECTOR

You planned to be worldly-wise
But your souls were dark.

ELLEN

We planned this time to
Care for the boy,
To save him from danger
And hardship sore . . .
And mending his clothes and giving him
Regular meals . . .

MRS SEDLEY

Oh, little care you for the prentice
Or his welfare!

BOLES

Call it danger, call it hardship,
Or plain murder!

NED

And thanks to flinty human hearts
Even quacks can make a profit.

SWALLOW

You planned to heal sick souls
With bodily care.

NIECES

Perhaps his clothes you mended
But you work his bones bare!

AUNTIE

You meant just to be kind,
And avert fear!

BALSTRODE

You interfering gossips, this
Is not your business.

HOBSON

Pity the boy!

ELLEN

Oh pity those who try to bring
A shadowed life into the sun.

ELLEN, AUNTIE AND BALSTRODE

Oh hard, hard hearts!

CHORUS

Who lets us down must take the rap,
The Borough keeps its standards up.

OMNES
(*without Ellen, Auntie and Balstrode*)

Ha, ha! Tried to be kind!
Murder!
Ha, ha! Tried to be kind and to help!
Murder!

RECTOR

Swallow! Shall we go and see Grimes in his
hut?

SWALLOW

Popular feeling's rising!

RECTOR

Balstrode. I'd like you to come.

BALSTRODE

I warn you. We shall waste our time.

RECTOR

I'd like your presence just the same!

MRS SEDLEY

Little do the suspects know,
I've the evidence. I've a clue.

NED, NIECES, HOBSON AND CHORUS

Now we will find out the worst.

SWALLOW
(*points to the nieces who join the crowd*)

No ragtail, no bobtail if you please!

BOLES
(*pushes them away*)

Back to the gutter – you keep out of this.

RECTOR

Only the men, the women stay!
Mr Swallow. Come along.

SWALLOW

Carter Hobson, fetch the drum.
Summon the Boro' to Grimes's hut.

CHORUS

To Grimes's hut!
To Grimes's hut!

*He leads the way. Mrs Sedley and Swallow
come next. Balstrode lags behind. Behind
them come the rest of the crowd.*

**MRS SEDLEY, BOLES, RECTOR, NED,
SWALLOW, CHORUS**

Now is gossip put on trial,
Now the rumours either fail,
Or are shouted in the wind,
Sweeping furious through the land.
Now the liars shiver for
Now if they've cheated we shall know!
We shall strike and strike to kill,
At the slander or the sin!
Now the whisperers stand out,
Now confronted by the fact . . .
Bring the branding iron and knife,
What's done now is done for life. Now.

Auntie, Nieces and Ellen remain.

NIECES [20]

From the gutter, why should we
Trouble at their ribaldries?

AUNTIE

And shall we be ashamed because
We comfort men from ugliness?

ALL FOUR

Do we smile or do we weep
Or wait quietly till they sleep?

AUNTIE

When in storm they shelter here,
And we soothe their fears away!

NIECES

We know they'll whistle their good-byes,
Next fine day and put to sea!

ELLEN

On the manly calendar
We only mark heroic days!

ALL FOUR

Do we smile or do we weep
Or wait quietly till they sleep?

ELLEN

They are children when they weep,
We are mothers when they strive,
Schooling our own hearts to keep
The bitter treasure of their love.

ALL FOUR

Do we smile or do we weep
Or wait quietly till they sleep?

Curtain.

Interlude IV: Passacaglia [21]

Scene Two. *Grimes's hut is an upturned boat. It is on the whole shipshape, though bare and forbidding. Ropes coiled, nets, kegs and casks furnish the place. It is lighted by a skylight. There are two doors, one (back centre) opens on the cliff, the other down-stage, opens on the road. The boy staggers into the room as if thrust from behind. Peter follows. He pulls down the boy's fishing clothes which were neatly stacked on a shelf.*

PETER

Go there!
Here's your sea boots! Take those bright
And fancy buckles off your feet!

He throws the sea boots down in front of the boy.

There's your oilskin and sou-wester.
Stir your pins, we must get ready.
Here's the jersey that she knitted,
With the anchor that she patterned.

He throws the clothes to the boy. They fall on the floor round him. The boy is crying silently. Peter shakes his shoulder.

I'll tear the collar off your neck!
Steady! Don't take fright, boy! Stop!

Peter opens the cliff-side door and looks out.

Look! Now is your chance!
The whole sea's boiling! Get the nets!

Come, boy!
They listen to money –
These Borough gossips,
Only to money.
I'll fish the sea dry,
Flood the market.
Now is our chance to get a good catch,
Get money to choke
Down rumour's throat.
I will set up –
With house and home and shop.
I'll marry Ellen, I'll . . .
I'll marry Ellen, I'll . . .

He turns to see the boy still sitting on the rope coil, weeping. He helps him off with his coat. He picks up the jersey.

Coat off! Jersey on!
My boy . . . We're going to sea.

The boy is still weeping. Peter changes tone and breaks into another song. [22]

In dreams I've built myself some kindlier home
Warm in my heart and in a golden calm
Where there'll be no more fear and no more storm.

And she will soon forget her schoolhouse ways,
Forget the labour of those weary days,
Wrapped round in kindness like September haze.

The learned at their books have no more store
Of wisdom than we'd close behind our door,
Compared with us the rich man would be poor.

I've seen in stars the life that we might share:
Fruit in the garden, children by the shore,
A whitened doorstep, and a woman's care!

But dreaming builds what dreaming can disown.
Dead fingers stretch themselves to tear it down.
I hear those voices that will not be drowned

Calling: there is no stone
In earth's thickness to make a home,
That you can build with and remain alone.

He stops. The boy watches him in fascinated horror, and Peter turns on him suddenly.

Sometimes I see that boy here in this hut.
He's there now, I can see him, he is there!
His eyes are on me as they were that evil day.

He stares into vacancy.

Stop moaning boy! Water?
There's no more water. You had the last yesterday.
You'll soon be home!
In harbour still and deep.

In the distance can be heard the song of the neighbours coming up the hill.

CHORUS
(off)

Now is gossip put on trial,
Now the rumours either fail,
Or are shouted in the wind,
Sweeping furious through the land.
Now the liars shiver for
Now if they've cheated we shall know.
We shall strike and strike to kill
At the slander or the sin!

Peter goes to the street door and looks out.

PETER

There's an odd procession here.
Parson and Swallow coming near.

CHORUS
(off)

Now the whisperers stand out,
Now confronted by the fact,
Bring the branding iron and knife,
What's done now is done for life.

The boy doesn't move. Peter flings the other door open. Suddenly he turns on the boy.

PETER

Wait! You've been talking!
You and that bitch were gossiping!
What lies have you been telling?
The Borough's climbing up the hill.
To get me. Me! Oh, I'm not scared.
I'll send them off with a flea in their ear.
I'll show them. Grimes ahoy!
You sit there watching me.
And you're the cause of everything.
Your eyes, like his, are watching me
With an idiot's drooling gaze!
Will you move
Or must I make you dance?

Step boldly! For here's the way we go to sea
To find that shoal, to find that shoal
That's boiling in the sea!
Careful, or you'll break your neck!
Down the cliff-side to the deck.

Rope in hand he drives the boy towards the cliff door.

I'll pitch the stuff down. Come on!

He pitches rope and nets.

Now . . .
Shut your eyes and down you go!

There is a knocking at the other door. Peter turns towards it, then retreats. Meanwhile the boy climbs out. When Peter is between the two doors the boy screams and falls out of sight. Peter runs to the cliff door, feels for his grip and then swings after him.

The cliff door is open. The street door still resounds with the Rector's knock. Then it opens and the Rector puts his head round the door.

RECTOR

Peter Grimes! Nobody here?

SWALLOW

What about the other door?

They go and look out. Silence for a moment.

RECTOR

Was this a recent landslide?

SWALLOW
                    Yes.

RECTOR

It makes almost a precipice.
How deep?

SWALLOW
        Say forty feet.

RECTOR

Dangerous to have the door open.

NED

He used to keep his boat down there,
Maybe they've both gone fishing.

RECTOR
                    Yet
His hut is reasonably kept,
Here's order, here's skill.

Swallow draws the moral.

SWALLOW

The whole affair gives Borough talk its –
    shall
I say – quietus? Here we come pell-mell
Expecting to find out – we know not what.
But all we find is a neat and empty hut.
Gentlemen, take this to your wives:
Less interference in our private lives.

RECTOR

There's no point certainly in staying here,
And will the last to go please close the door.

They go out – all save Balstrode, who has come in late, and who goes to the cliff side door, looks down, then closes it carefully.

Curtain.

Act Three

Scene One. *Scene as in Act One, a few days later.*

The time is summer evening. One of the season's subscription dances is taking place in the Moot Hall which is brightly lit and from which we can hear the band playing a polka and the rhythm of the dancers' feet. The Boar too is brightly lit and, as the dance goes on there will be a regular passage – of the males at any rate – from the Moot Hall to the inn.

The stage is empty when the curtain rises but presently there is a little squeal and one of the nieces scampers down the exterior staircase of the Moot Hall, closely followed by Swallow. They haven't got very far before the other niece appears at the top of the Moot Hall stairs.

A barn dance is being played in the Moot Hall.

SWALLOW
(to 1st Niece)

Assign your prettiness to me,
I'll seal the deed and take no fee;
My signature, your graceful mark
Are witnessed by the abetting dark.

BOTH NIECES

Together we are safe
As any wedded wife
For safety in number lies.
A man is always lighter,
His conversation's brighter,
Provided that the tête-à-tête's in threes.

SWALLOW

Assign your prettiness to me,
I'll call it real property.
Your sister shan't insist upon
Her stay of execution!

NIECES

Save us from lonely men,
They're like a broody hen!
With habits but with no ideas.
But in their choice of pleasures
They show their coloured feathers
Provided that the tête-à-tête's in threes.

SWALLOW

I shall take steps to change her mind;
She has first option on my love.
If my appeal should be ignored
I'll take it to the House of Lords!

NIECES

Oh, pairing's all to blame
For awkwardness and shame,

And all these manly sighs and tears,
Which wouldn't be expended
If people condescended
Always to have their tête-à-tête's in threes!

SWALLOW

Assign your prettiness to me,
We'll make an absolute decree
Of quiet enjoyment which you'll bless
By sending sister somewhere else!

2ND NIECE

Ned Keene is chasing me, gives me no peace!

SWALLOW

He went to The Boar to have a glass;
Sister and I will join him there!
If you don't want Ned you'd better stay
here.

He opens the inn door. Niece is about to enter when –

1ST NIECE

They're all watching. I must wait
Until Auntie's turned her back!

She runs away to join her sister and leaves Swallow holding the door open.

SWALLOW

Bah!

He goes in The Boar alone. The barn dance stops – applause. The sisters are half-way upstairs when Ned Keene comes out of the Moot Hall at the top of the stairs. They fly, giggling, and hide behind one of the boats by the shore. (Three boats can be seen, as at the end of Act One.)

NED
(calls after them)

Ahoy!

He is halfway to their hiding place when a peremptory voice stops him in mid-career. Mrs Sedley is at the top of the Moot Hall stairs. A slow waltz starts from the Moot Hall.

MRS SEDLEY

Mr Keene! Can you spare a moment?
I've something to say that's more than
urgent!
About Peter Grimes and that boy.

She is downstairs by now and has him buttonholed.

Neither of them was seen yesterday.
It's more than suspicion now, it's fact.
The boy's disappeared.

NED

Do you expect me to act
Like a Bow Street runner or a constable?

MRS SEDLEY

At least you can trouble to hear what
I've got to say!
For two days I've kept my eyes open;
For two days I've said nothing,
Only watched and taken notes,
Pieced clue to clue, and bit by bit
Reconstructed all the crime.
Everything points to Peter Grimes:
He is the murderer!

NED [23]

Old woman, you're far too ready
To yell 'blue murder'.
If people poke their noses into others'
     business –
No! They won't get me to help them –
They'll find there's merry hell to pay!
You just tell me where's the body?

MRS SEDLEY

In the sea the prentice lies,
Whom nobody has seen for days!
Murder most foul it is,
Eerie I find it,
My skin's a prickly heat,
Blood cold behind it!
In midnight's loneliness
And thrilling quiet
The history I trace,
The stifling secret.
Murder most foul it is . . .
And I'll declare it!

NED
(*who is getting bored, thirsty and angry*)

Are you mad, old woman,
Or is it too much laudanum?

MRS SEDLEY
(*like a cross-examining counsel*)

Has Peter Grimes been seen?

NED

He's away.

MRS SEDLEY

And the boy?

NED

They're fishing, likely.

MRS SEDLEY

Has his boat been in?

NED

Why should it?

MRS SEDLEY

His hut's abandoned.

NED

I'm dry, goodnight.

The waltz stops. He breaks away from her grasp, goes into The Boar and bangs the door after him. Dr Crabbe and the Rector and other burgesses come down the Moot Hall stairs. Mrs Sedley retires into the shadow of the boats. A hornpipe starts from the Moot Hall.

BURGESS

Come along doctor –
         (*indicates The Boar*)
We're not wanted there, we oldsters.

BURGESSES

Good night – it's time for bed.
Good night! Good night! Good night, good
     people, good night!

RECTOR

I looked in a moment, the company's gay,
With pretty young women and youths on
     the spree;
So parched like my roses, but now the
     sun's down,
I'll water my roses and leave you the wine!

BURGESSES

Good night! Good night! Good night, good
     people, good night!

RECTOR

Good night, Dr Crabbe, all good friends
     goodnight.
Don't let the ladies keep company too late!
My love to the maidens, wish luck to the
     men,
I'll water my roses and leave you the wine.

He goes out waving.

BURGESSES

Good night! Good night! Good night, good
     people, good night!

The hornpipe fades out.

MRS SEDLEY
(*still in the boat shadow, goes on with her brooding.*)

Crime, which my hobby is,
Sweetens my thinking;
Men who can breach the peace
And kill convention –
So many guilty ghosts,
With stealthy body
Trouble my midnight thoughts . . .

Ellen and Balstrode come up slowly from the beach. It is clear they have been in earnest talk. As they approach Balstrode shines his lantern on the name of the nearest boat: 'Boy Billy'. Mrs Sedley doesn't show herself.

ELLEN

Is the boat in?

BALSTRODE

Yes! For more than an hour.
Peter seems to have disappeared
Not in his boat, not in his hut.

ELLEN
(*holds out the boy's jersey*)

This I found
Down by the tide-mark.

*It is getting dark. To see the garment
properly Balstrode holds it to his lantern.*

BALSTRODE

The boy's!

ELLEN

My broidered anchor on the chest
(*meditative*) [24]
Embroidery in childhood was
A luxury of idleness.
A coil of silken thread giving
Dreams of silk and satin life.
Now my broidery affords
The clue whose meaning we avoid.

My hand remembered its old skill –
These stitches tell a curious tale.
I remember I was brooding
On the fantasies of children
And dreamt that only by wishing I
Could bring some silk into their lives.
Now my broidery affords
The clue whose meaning we avoid.

*The jersey is wet. Balstrode wrings the water
out.*

BALSTRODE

We'll find him, maybe give him a hand.

ELLEN

We have no power to help him now.

BALSTRODE

We have the power. We have the power.

In the black moment
When your friend suffers
Unearthly torment,
We cannot turn our backs.
When horror breaks one heart,
All hearts are broken.

ELLEN

We shall be there with him.

BALSTRODE

Nothing to do but wait
Since the solution
Is beyond life, beyond
Dissolution.

*They go out together. When they have gone
Mrs Sedley goes quickly to the inn door.*

MRS SEDLEY
(*calling through the door*)

Mr Swallow! Mr Swallow!
I want the lawyer Swallow!

AUNTIE
(*off*)

What do you want?

MRS SEDLEY

I want the lawyer Swallow!

AUNTIE

He's busy!

MRS SEDLEY

Fetch him please, this is official.
Business about the Boro' criminal.
Please do as I tell you!

AUNTIE

My customers come here for peace,
For quiet, away from you,
And all such nuisances!

MRS SEDLEY

This is an insult!

AUNTIE

You'll find
So long as I am here, you'll find
That I always speak my mind.

MRS SEDLEY

I'll have you know your place,
You baggage!

AUNTIE

My customers come here,
They take their drink, they take their ease!

SWALLOW
(*coming out*)

Hi! What's the matter?

AUNTIE
(*goes in and bangs the door*)

Good night!

MRS SEDLEY
(*points dramatically*)

Look!

SWALLOW

I'm short-sighted, you know.

MRS SEDLEY

It's Grimes's boat, back at last!

SWALLOW

That's different. Hey!
(*shouting into The Boar*)
Is Hobson there?

56

HOBSON
(off)

Ay, Ay, sir!

MRS SEDLEY

Good, now things are moving; and about
time too!

Hobson appears.

SWALLOW

You're constable of the Borough,
Carter Hobson.

HOBSON

Ay, Ay, sir!

SWALLOW

As the mayor,
I ask you to find Peter Grimes.
Take whatever help you need.

HOBSON

Now what I claims
Is he's out at sea.

SWALLOW
(points)

But here's his boat.

HOBSON

Oh! We'll send a posse to his hut.

SWALLOW

If he's not there, you'll search the shore,
The marsh, the fields, the streets, the
    Borough.

HOBSON

Ay, Ay, sir!
Here, there! Hey! Come out and help!
Grimes is around! Hey! Hey, there!
Come on! Come on! Come on! Come on!

He goes into The Boar hailing.

MRS SEDLEY

Crime – that's my hobby – is
By cities hoarded.
Rarely are country minds
Lifted to murder,
The noblest of the crimes
Which are my study.
And now the crime is here
And I am ready!

*Hobson comes out with Boles and other
fishermen. When the news reaches the Moot
Hall and pub, the people crowd on to the
beach.*

CHORUS

Who holds himself apart
Let's his pride rise.
Him who despises us
We'll destroy!

**WITH TWO NIECES, MRS SEDLEY, BOLES,
KEENE, SWALLOW, HOBSON**

And cruelty becomes
His enterprise;
Him who despises us,   [25]
We'll destroy.

Our curse shall fall on his evil day;
We shall tame his arrogance!
Ha! Ha! Ha!
We'll make the murderer pay for his crime.

Peter Grimes! Grimes!

*The people, still shouting, scatter in all
directions.*

Curtain.

Interlude VI

Scene Two. *Scene as in Scene One. Some
hours later.*

*The dance is over, the Borough is out
hunting. Peter alone by his boat in the
changeful light of a cloud-swept moon.
There is a distant fog-horn. The orchestra is
silent. As before we can hear shouting, now
in the far distance:* 'Peter Gri-imes – Peter
Gri-imes.'

VOICES

Grimes!

PETER

Steady. There you are. Nearly home.
What is home? Calm as deep water.
Where's my home? Deep in calm water.
Water will drink my sorrows dry,
And the tide will turn.

VOICES

Grimes!

PETER

Steady! There you are! Nearly home!
The first one died, just died . . .
The other slipped, and died . . .
And the third will . . .
'Accidental circumstances' . . .
Water will drink his sorrows . . .
My sorrows dry,
And the tide will turn.

VOICES

Grimes, Peter Grimes!

PETER

Peter Grimes! Here you are! Here I am!
Hurry, hurry!
Now is gossip put on trial.
Bring the branding iron, the knife . . .
What's done now is done for life . . .
Come on! Land me!
'Turn the skies back and begin again!'

VOICES

Peter Grimes!

PETER

'Old Joe had gone fishing and
Young Joe has gone fishing and
You'll know who's gone fishing when
You land the next shoal.'

VOICES

Grimes!

PETER

Ellen! Give me your hand.
There now – my hope is held by you . . .
If you leave me alone,
If you take away your hand . . .
The argument's finished,
Friendship is lost,
Gossip is shouting,
Everything's said.

VOICES

Peter Grimes!

PETER

To hell with all your mercy!
To hell with your revenge,
And God have mercy upon you!

VOICES

Peter Grimes! Peter Grimes!

PETER

Do you hear them all shouting my name?
D'you hear them?
Old Davy Jones shall answer:
Come home, come home.

VOICES
(*close at hand*)

Peter Grimes!

PETER
(*roars back at them*)

Peter Grimes! Peter Grimes!

Ellen and Balstrode have come in and stand watching. Then Ellen goes up to Peter.

ELLEN

Peter, we've come to take you home.
Oh, come home out of this dreadful night!
See, here's Balstrode. Peter, don't you hear me?

Peter does not notice her and sings in a tone almost like prolonged sobbing. The voices shouting 'Peter Grimes' can still be heard but more distantly and more sweetly.

PETER

What harbour shelters peace,
Away from tidal waves,
Away from storms!
What harbour can embrace

Terrors and tragedies?
Her breast is harbour too –
Where night is turned to day.

BALSTRODE
(*He goes up to Peter and speaks.*)

Come on, I'll help you with the boat.

ELLEN

No!

BALSTRODE

Sail out till you lose sight of the Moot Hall,
then sink the boat. D'you hear? Sink her.
Good-bye Peter.

Together they push the boat down the slope of the shore. Balstrode comes back and waves goodbye. He takes Ellen, who is sobbing quietly, calms her and leads her carefully down the main street home. The men pushing the boat out has been the cue for the orchestra to return. Now dawn begins.

Dawn comes to the Borough by a gentle sequence of sights and sounds.

A candle is lighted and shines through a bare window. A shutter is drawn back.

Hobson and his posse meet severally on the green by the Moot Hall. They gossip together, shake their heads, indicate the hopelessness of the search, extinguish their lanterns, and while some turn home, others go to the boats.

Nets are brought down from the houses by fisherwives. Cleaners open the front door of the inn and begin to scrub the step.

Dr Crabbe comes from a confinement case with his black bag. He yawns and stretches. Nods to the cleaners. The Rector comes to early morning prayer. Mrs Sedley follows. Ned Keene draws the shutters of his shop. Mrs Swallow comes out and speaks to the fishermen.

Nieces emerge and begin to polish the brasses outside The Boar.

CHORUS

To those who pass, the Boro' sounds betray
The cold beginning of another day,
And houses sleeping by the waterside
Wake to the measured ripple of the tide.

SWALLOW

There's a boat sinking out at sea,
Coastguard reports.

FISHERMAN

Within reach?

SWALLOW

No.

FISHERMAN

Let's have a look through the glasses.

*Fishermen go with Swallow to the beach
and look out. One of them has a glass.*

CHORUS

Or measured cadence of the lads who tow
Some entered hoy to fix her in her row.
Or hollow sound that from the passing bell
To some departed spirit bids farewell.

AUNTIE

What is it?

BOLES

Nothing I can see.

AUNTIE

One of these rumours.

CHORUS

In ceaseless motion comes and goes the tide,
Flowing it fills the channel broad and wide,
Then back to sea with strong majestic sweep
It rolls in ebb yet terrible and deep.

During the Chorus the curtain slowly falls.

*Covent Garden, 1975: Geraint Evans (Balstrode) and Jon Vickers (Grimes) (photo: Clive
Barda)*

59

Joan Cross with a model of a woman of the time and place given her by the photographer, Angus McBean (photo: Angus McBean)

Kenneth Green's set for 'Peter Grimes' at Sadler's Wells in 1945

'Peter Grimes' and 'Gloriana'

*Joan Cross CBE and Sir Peter Pears CBE
in conversation with John Evans*

JOAN CROSS can be said to have had two distinguished performing careers: pre-war and post-war. Though this was perhaps not unique among artists of her generation, whose careers were interrupted by war service, very few chose to rechannel their talents in the service of new music as she was to do in her close association with Benjamin Britten as a founder artist of the English Opera Group and the Aldeburgh Festival.

She joined the Old Vic Company (which later was to become the Sadler's Wells Opera) in the 1923-4 season as a member of the chorus. Gifted with a touchingly beautiful voice of the lyrico-spinto variety (with that quality described by Italians as *morbidezza*) she became the leading soprano of the company, singing a wide variety of roles, for instance in *The Marriage of Figaro*, *La Traviata*, *Tannhäuser*, *Lohengrin*, *The Valkyrie*, *Carmen*, *Otello* and *Der Rosenkavalier*. During the war she toured initially with a small company of Sadler's Wells artists all over the country and then helped to keep the company alive by undertaking its management at a time when its very existence was threatened. She sang very seldom during these years — an occasional Butterfly or Violetta and at the end of the war a superb Fiordiligi in *Così fan tutte* — and considered her repertory career to have been brought to an early end. In 1945, in the closing months of the war in Europe, she convinced the Administrators of the Old Vic and Sadler's Wells that it would be altogether admirable to reopen the theatre in Rosebery Avenue with the world première of Benjamin Britten's first opera, *Peter Grimes*. At Britten's insistence she sang the role of Ellen Orford in that première, which proved to be the watershed of her post-war career with the English Opera Group. Britten composed the roles of Female Chorus in *The Rape of Lucretia*, Lady Billows in *Albert Herring*, and Mrs Grose in *The Turn of the Screw* especially for her, and in June 1953 she created the title role in Britten's Coronation opera, *Gloriana*, in a gala at the Royal Opera House, Covent Garden. During this period she also founded and directed the National School of Opera at Morley College. She now lives in Suffolk and continues her association with the Britten legacy as a guest teacher at the Britten-Pears School for Advanced Musical Studies at Snape Maltings.

PETER PEARS began his lifelong association with Benjamin Britten in 1937, when he and the composer first gave recitals together. After a three-year period in North America, Britten and Pears returned to the UK in 1942 at the height of the Second World War. Both were convinced pacifists and appeared before a Tribunal as committed conscientious objectors and were exempted from military service. Pears joined Sadler's Wells Opera in 1943, singing leading roles in *The Magic Flute*, *Rigoletto*, *The Bartered Bride*, *La Traviata*, *The Barber of Seville* and *Così fan tutte* during the war, and creating the title role in the première of *Peter Grimes* at Sadler's Wells on June 7, 1945. Thereafter his close relationship with Britten proved a powerful source of inspiration for the composer; a vast quantity of music — including thirteen operatic roles (from Grimes to Gustav von Aschenbach in *Death in Venice* (1973)), song-cycles (with piano and with orchestra), five canticles and solo parts in major choral works such at *St Nicolas* (1948), *Spring Symphony* (1949) and *War Requiem* (1961) — was composed specifically for Pears. In 1953 he created the role of the Earl of Essex in *Gloriana*. He was a founder artist of the English Opera Group in 1947, a founder Artistic Director (with Britten and Eric Crozier) of the Aldeburgh Festival in 1948 and Founder-Director of the Britten-Pears School for Advanced Musical Studies in 1972.

I interviewed Miss Cross and Sir Peter at the Red House in Aldeburgh, Sir Peter's home with Benjamin Britten since 1957. Since Britten's death in 1976 Sir Peter has continued to live at the Red House where he observes with sometimes amused and sometimes astonished eyes, the considerable development of the Britten-Pears Library and the Britten Archive. The interview that follows was undertaken in informal circumstances and we have attempted to retain the atmosphere of the original transcript of our taped conversation.

May 1983

John Evans

I began by asking Sir Peter to recall the incidents that led to Britten's choosing George Crabbe's *The Borough*, and specifically the story of the fisherman, Peter Grimes, as the subject of his first opera.

PETER PEARS: We were staying in Escondido on the West Coast of America with Rae Robertson and Ethel Bartlett, the pianists for whom Ben wrote the *Scottish Ballad*. It was at this time that we read Morgan Forster's article in the *Listener* about George Crabbe[1] and we were touched and interested enough to seek out a copy of Crabbe's poems and I well remember my surprise in discovering a mid-19th-century edition in San Diego, I think. And almost at once we started work on the Crabbe. By that time we were really longing to get back to England. We drove back across the States at the end of the summer of 1941 and then waited until we could get a passage home, which wasn't until the following March.

JOAN CROSS: And at that time *Grimes* was occupying your minds?

PP: Well, it was certainly at the back of our minds when we went to hear Koussevitzky[2] conduct Ben's *Sinfonia da Requiem* in Boston in January 1942. But it wasn't until Koussevitzky offered a commission of a thousand dollars from the Koussevitzky Music Foundation that Ben was seriously able to contemplate setting aside all the time that is required to write a full-scale opera.

JOHN EVANS: You started work on *Grimes* while still in America, didn't you?

PP: Yes. We started the first rough outline of a scenario. Then in March we travelled back to England on the *Axel Johnson*, a Swedish cargo boat with some passenger accommodation.

    We took four or five weeks to get across the Atlantic, being pursued by enemy submarines — all very worrying! — and while Ben was setting Auden's *Hymn to St Cecilia* and writing *A Ceremony of Carols* I started to put the *Grimes* scenario into shape.

JE: Did this scenario differ substantially from the opera as we now know it?

PP: Initially we had a prologue in which Peter Grimes's father appeared on his death-bed, in which he solemnly cursed his son; but it became apparent fairly soon that this was not a very good idea and the prologue was reshaped by the time we arrived back in England.[3]

JE: Had you, at this time, any ambitions to write the libretto yourself, Peter?

PP: I really didn't think of myself as being capable of writing a libretto. I'm not a man of all that much letters, though I like to think that I was fully capable of arranging Shakespeare for Ben's *A Midsummer Night's Dream*. While we were still in America Ben had approached Christopher Isherwood[4] about *Grimes*, but that collaboration was obviously not going to be feasible when we decided to return to England. When we arrived home Ben asked Montagu Slater to write the libretto; he was a playwright and had worked in films, and Ben had written incidental music for a number of his Left Theatre productions, including a very well-received play called *Stay Down Miner*, during the thirties. During the war Montagu worked for the Ministry of Information in the film division. He was based in London and Ben felt he would be sympathetic to the subject. As it turned out it was hard work one way and another because Montagu was not very prolific. He was a very slow writer and found it very difficult to produce what Ben wanted, so the actual work of the libretto was often well behind the work of the music. I remember ghastly evenings when we sat round willing him to write half a line or finish a stanza and he couldn't do it, it wouldn't come out.

JC: I wonder how far the piece had progressed when I engaged you to come and sing with Sadler's Wells Opera in January 1943? I seem to remember that the first information I ever had about Ben was that he had measles! At the same time I became aware of the fact that this opera was on the stocks.

JE: Had you heard much of Britten's music by this time, Joan?

JC: I regret to say no. That is until I was invited with Lawrance Collingwood[5] to the Wigmore Hall and heard Peter perform *Les Illuminations* [May 15 1943]. And we were stunned. *I* had no idea that a composer could conjure the sounds of trumpets, horns and trombones from a string orchestra. Following this I also heard the first performance of the *Serenade* with Peter and Dennis Brain at the Wigmore Hall in October 1943.

JE: And Peter was by now in the company?

JC: Yes. When he auditioned for us, late in '42, Collingwood's reaction was 'a marvellous musician!', but at the same time Menges[6] was concerned that his voice wouldn't carry in the larger theatres. But, of course, I was determined to take him into the company and his first role for us was Tamino in *Magic Flute*. Then he joined the cast of *Barber of Seville*, *Bartered Bride*, *Traviata* and *Così fan tutte*.

JE: What were the circumstances of the company during the war?

JC: During the first year of the war a somewhat depleted company continued to perform at Sadler's Wells (Rosebery Avenue). But on September 7, during a matinée of *Tosca* and an evening performance of *Faust*, the docks were attacked and the blitz began. Of course, all theatrical activities came to an abrupt halt; but Guthrie[7] was not prepared to accept what seemed like being the total demise of Sadler's Wells Opera, and proposed sending a small touring group of the company round the provinces and he offered me a small contract. I was happy to accept. We began a more than modest tour in Buxton in October 1940 and continued touring all over the country, with occasional visits to the Prince's Theatre or the New Theatre [now the Albery] in London, until the war ended.

JE: At what stage did you decide to première *Peter Grimes* at Sadler's Wells?

JC: I remember Ben arrived in Liverpool with his score and played parts of the opera to me. I became at once *possessive* about it . . . there was already talk about the war ending and Sadler's Wells reopening and it seemed to me entirely fitting for the Sadler's Wells Company to reopen the theatre at Rosebery Avenue after the war with a new opera by a leading young English composer. But there were difficulties. Boosey and Hawkes[8] were not, at first, terribly willing to co-operate. They owned the lease of Covent Garden and had plans to reopen the Opera House and stage *Grimes* there. And Ralph Hawkes,[9] who was a splendid person and a very good friend, was not prepared to extend friendship to this degree and allow the piece to be done in Sadler's Wells, and he took a lot of persuading.

JE: How were you able to overcome these difficulties with Britten's publisher?

JC: Ben took it into his own hands. He had decided that Sadler's Wells was where he wanted the first performance. He realized that it could be ideally cast within the existing company.

JE: But, ironically, the members of the company were none too keen on the prospect of staging *Peter Grimes*, were they?

JC: At the time there was a lot of discontent in the company. They had had four years' grind up and down the country with uncomfortable lodgings, often very bad theatres and performing the same limited repertoire week after week, month after month. They wanted to reopen Sadler's Wells with *Carmen, Aida, Trovatore*, operas they hadn't been able to perform during the war. And here they were faced with this strange opera, the plot of which they found unattractive, the music very difficult and, indeed, unrecognizable in any way at all as operatic music as they understood it. I received a letter from one of the repetiteurs informing me emphatically that the chorus thought the music was very bad for their voices. One sympathized, but how they failed to recognize the extraordinary quality of the work will always be beyond me.

JE: Was there, in a sense, a policy decision on the part of the management, to give the younger generation of producers and conductors the responsibility for the première of *Grimes*?

JC: Eric Crozier[10] had had a great success producing *The Bartered Bride*. He admired Ben and seemed to get on well with him. I suggested to Ben that he might produce *Grimes* and Ben, having seen *The Bartered Bride* and, I think, enjoyed it, agreed. And then it was a question of who was to conduct the piece. Collingwood felt that it was a young man's opera and suggested Reggie.[11]

PP: Reggie was marvellous. No one has ever conducted the big man-hunt scene as well as he. No one!

JC: Kenneth Green[12] had designed our production of *Così fan tutte* which had been a great success. His *Grimes* was really quite a nice piece of work.

PP: I thought the enclosed, claustrophobic quality of his set was absolutely right for the Borough.

JE: In what respects do you consider your interpretations of the roles of Ellen and Peter to have differed from more recent exponents of these roles?

JC: Most of the opera repertoire is written for younger singers. Ellen Orford in the poem is a middle-aged woman and it was fortuitous for me that I was about the right age — it's not a part for a *young* soprano. I always regarded Ellen's attitude towards Grimes as one of sympathy and understanding and a desire to help him out of his difficulties. She has a deep regard for him and a feeling that here is a poet, a man that nobody understands.

PP: He, in turn, merely envisages a peaceful orderly life that, with her help, *could* be possible.

JC: Of course, in Crabbe's *The Borough* she is blind. I once asked Ben, 'Would you like her to be blind? I could do this if you like.' He was horrified! It could be possible, but unbearably pathetic. Grimes couldn't possibly hit a blind woman, could he?

PP: No, he wouldn't have done that.

JC: Peter, in fact could never ever bring himself to hit Ellen, blind or otherwise. I remember a perfectly exhausting rehearsal with Guthrie and Peter, Guthrie persuading, saying, 'It doesn't hurt her really — *slap, wallop* — you do that.' Peter would go so far and then no further, till I was bright scarlet from Guthrie's ministrations and nothing from Peter. Oh dear!

PP: I think most of the time I *didn't* hit you, I just hit the air.
     You were saying, Joan, that you regard Grimes as a poet in a way. And of course that is specially true and where one differs frequently from one's successors.

JC: Surely this is the difficulty with the part. The man is such an incredible mixture, and so fascinating. 'The Great Bear and Pleiades' — this is pure poetry and it flows out of him. Whether he's aware of it is another matter altogether. What do you think?

PP: Grimes is in full reaction against his environment. While he cannot really be called a poet, he has strong and sensitive feelings which show themselves in poetic music in the opera. Essentially he is frustrated and releases his frustration by careless and violent action.

JC: I remember I used to take great pleasure in performing in the Prologue. I don't know whether it contributed much — one never knows oneself whether it contributes or not — but I *never* took my eyes off Peter during this scene, willed him to do this, that and the other, and was saddened and grieved and distressed by the fact that everybody turned against him at the end.

PP: And the duet at the end of the Prologue is a very touching moment.

JC: It also happens to be very difficult to sing.
     The other passage that makes a most extraordinary effect emotionally is Ellen's exit after she agrees to go and collect the new apprentice for Grimes. The succession of downward phrases in the orchestra is *so* moving. Time after time I used to land up off the stage in tears. I cannot tell you why. It had such incredible dignity and power, and it was something that made these villagers, these people who were being so tiresome, give way to her as she walked through them, and it's in the *music*.

JE: Though this role was written for you, in a sense, did you find it difficult having to sing Britten after a long career in the standard repertoire?

JC: Ben didn't write this role for me. No, he didn't really know my voice.

PP: That's not quite true. From 1943 onwards he probably didn't miss a single performance in which I was taking part and he must have seen us in *Traviata* every time it was done. And he came to our performances of *Così*.

JC: That's interesting, because I've often wondered whether *'Come scoglio'* gave him ideas. All those wide leaps and difficult intervals in the Mozart could just have influenced his writing of the 'Embroidery' Aria.

And isn't the women's quartet a remarkable piece of music? It has the same kind of surprising beauty as the trio at the end of *Rosenkavalier*.

JE: It's interesting that you should mention *Rosenkavalier* in this context, because while Britten was in hospital with measles, during the period when he was writing *Grimes*, Ralph Hawkes sent him a score of *Rosenkavalier*. And though the women's quartet in *Grimes* is a quartet of voices, it is more often in three-part counterpoint because the Nieces sing in unison in the refrain.

PP: Yes, quite extraordinary. I remember very well Ben's insistence that he wanted to retain that quartet. Originally it wasn't there at all. And he said that we'd got to have some softening, some change, some relaxation after the intensity of the march to the hut. I remember also the reaction of one or two of Ben's older contemporaries, Constant Lambert and Patrick Hadley, who were particularly touched by this quartet when they first heard it at the dress rehearsal.

JC: And it's wonderful stuff to sing. And nothing could be more marvellous to sing than parts of the church scene. [Sings:] 'Were we mistaken when we schemed . . .' Glorious phrase! And the interruptions from Grimes and the orchestra are so staggeringly dramatic. It is a work that could have been written by a man who'd been writing operas for twenty years and it introduced me to Ben's remarkable sense of theatre. A pity it was launched really under unhappy circumstances inasmuch as the company was so antipathetic. It didn't make a great occasion for me, though I think the backstage tension did contribute something to the success of the production. But it made it a very anxious first night for me, and before the curtain went up, as I sat in my dressing-room in make-up and costume ready to go on stage, Guthrie, who'd been really very sympathetic if not totally convinced all along, came in, patted me on the shoulder and said, 'Whatever happens, dear, we were right to do it.'

JE: As it turned out, *Peter Grimes* was a very great success, despite the tensions that surrounded its première. *Gloriana*, by contrast, was launched in the most auspicious of circumstances but seemed to be one of Britten's most upsetting professional disappointments.[13]

PP: It was absolutely fatal, of course, to have made a royal gala out of the first night. Quite fatal! That was really the trouble.

JC: What I remember about the first night was an uncomfortable feeling that the piece was under-rehearsed musically.

PP: You may be quite right about that, because something intensified the first-night nerves, not only because of the artificiality of the occasion.

JC: Would you agree, Peter, that there was a feeling at this time that Ben was receiving too much attention and that there was a kind of resentment kicking about amongst musicians?

PP: It could have been so. Ben had been made a Companion of Honour in the Coronation Honours List and the very fact that he was writing an opera for the Coronation created jealousy in some quarters. But what was hoped for by many was a kind of superior *Merrie England*. This story about an ageing monarch was considered quite unsuitable for the young Queen at the start of her reign.

JE: Were you made painfully aware of the lack of interest of that first-night

The Royal Opera House decorated by Oliver Messel for the Coronation Gala in 1953 with (left to right) HM Queen Elizabeth II, HRH the Duke of Edinburgh and HM Queen Elizabeth the Queen Mother at the centre of the Royal Box. (Royal Opera House Archives)

audience, made up of monarchs and dignitaries 'commanded' to the performance as part of the Coronation celebrations?

PP: It was such an unusual relationship with the audience. It was almost like performing to an empty house.

JC: It really was quite an experience to sing to such an audience! At most, fifteen per cent were musical and able to appreciate the work. It was a relief to find that the reaction to the first public performance at Covent Garden contradicted the impression that the command performance had been a disaster.[14]

JE: Peter, was there never any possibility of Britten conducting the première?

PP: No, he'd more or less crippled himself with bursitis after four months of conducting *Billy Budd*.[15] It was the first big opera he'd conducted and he just didn't know how to do that, how to pace himself. Incidentally he did the same thing when we recorded *Peter Grimes* and Reggie had to come in and help finish the recording.

JE: But, presumably, he worked with you both individually?

JC: Oh yes, that was for me a very great joy. I stayed in Aldeburgh for some weeks in order to work with Ben whenever he had time. Viola Tunnard[16] came and stayed and was very, very helpful. She bullied me. I had begun to find it very difficult, at that stage of my life, to memorize new music.

JE: What was Britten striving for in these sessions?

JC: He was after a *musical* performance, but, as always, he was deeply interested in the characterization and the theatrical dimension of the role. His remarkable understanding of the stage made him immensely stimulating. The historical period is so well documented it was only necessary to read what had been written about Elizabeth and integrate it with Ben's score.[17]

PP: I do think that Ben's treatment of that last scene, at the end of the opera, was something that was quite new . . .[18]

JC: . . . suddenly having to stop singing and launch into speech . . .

PP: . . . terribly difficult to project into a vast theatre.

JC: I regret that so much of the spoken word is now cut.[19] It was one of Ben's innovations that I greatly enjoyed. I well remember, when rehearsing this piece, that Basil Coleman[20] took immense trouble persuading me to use enough voice. When I came to rehearse this scene with him, we went through it and he said to me, 'That won't do, you know,' and I was shattered. He said, 'You've really got to make a big speaking sound.' So we worked at it: he went to one end of a huge rehearsal room while I stood yelling at him from the other. Those speeches are remarkable in that they're *echt*, you know, they are historically recorded and accurately transcribed in the libretto.

But Gloriana herself is an extraordinary person, she's a dual-personality: on the one hand the public image, crisp, incisive, brusque, dismissive and intensely regal; on the other hand, the private nature, vulnerable, lyrical . . .

JE: And the strong rhythmic profile of much of her music enables the singer to create a direct impression of her public image . . .

JC: Precisely. The lyricism looks after itself.

JE: Am I right in saying, Peter, that you didn't feel entirely well cast as Essex?

PP: I adored the lute songs, of course, and there are two wonderful duets with Elizabeth, but I think that in many ways in the rest of the part I was wrongly cast. I'm not sure, but I think somebody else should have done it rather than me.

JE: Do you remember when the idea of a Coronation opera was first mooted?

PP: Yes. Ben and I had just given a recital in Vienna. That would have been in March 1952. We were joined there by George and Marion[21] and we all went off to a ski-ing resort called Gargellen. George VI had died in February and the subject of the Coronation inevitably cropped up.

JE: It was the Earl of Harewood who approached the Palace with the proposal of a Coronation opera by Britten, was it not? His cousin was the Queen's Private Secretary.[22]

PP: Of course, George was the obvious person to start the wheels turning. But Ben was already planning a children's opera with William Plomer to be called *Tyco the Vegan*. There were wonderful names in it, including a woman called Madge Plato. It was a sort of story that started with an aeroplane made by children in a garage. They managed to get it going, then took off and landed on a star. It was a dear idea, terribly sweet. But, of course, Ben had to drop that idea in order to write *Gloriana*.

JE: Presumably it's for this reason that he asked Plomer to collaborate on *Gloriana* instead.

JC: Peter, do you remember that really worrying evening when you, Ben, William and I were invited to a dinner party by the Harewoods at Orme Square [May 18, 1953]? The Queen and the Duke of Edinburgh were to be there and the Queen requested that she should hear some of *Gloriana*.

PP: William went through the story and described each scene . . .

JC: . . . and you and I performed bits and pieces from the opera with Ben at the piano. Not my favourite evening. I don't think *they* enjoyed the evening any more than we did.

JE: Joan, were you at all reluctant to take on this major role so late in your career?

JC: Reluctant, yes. I appreciated the very great honour of being asked — Coronation opera and all that — but I knew that my voice had been punished mercilessly during the war and I had, indeed, decided to retire from the opera stage.

PP: You had every right to retire if you wanted to, but of course we also had the right to try and persuade you not to. I agree that *Gloriana* was a considerable challenge.

JC: Yes, it's not an easy piece. Let's face it, none of Ben's pieces are easy. But I found the tessitura very awkward here and there. Ben never seemed to make up his mind whether I was a contralto or a soprano.

JE: Yes, much of the music he wrote for you, for instance the Female Chorus in *The Rape of Lucretia*, lies very low, particularly the slumber song that precedes the rape.

PP: Of course, Ben always challenged the artists he wrote for, extended them and offered new insights into the capabilities of their own voices or instruments.

JC: Whether he overestimated my capabilities or not, I'm pleased to have sung Gloriana, and enjoyed later performances conducted by my dear friend Reggie on the Covent Garden tour and during a visit to Rhodesia [Zimbabwe] for the Rhodes Festival in 1953. I'm more than delighted that more recent revivals have reinstated the work to its rightful place in the repertoire. As Guthrie foresaw and wrote to me after attending an early performance:

> I feel confident that *Gloriana* will survive and be considered a great work . . . that disastrous miscalculation of opening it to an audience and on an occasion that required an all-star *Iolanthe* will set it back twenty years. But one has to try and remember that's not important. The work, I think, crystallized an important change in operatic style which Ben is pioneering, texturally quite different — spiky, transparent, and a radically different conception of what theatre music should be. I know nothing of orchestration, but I have two ears (which is two more than the professional critics seem to have). . . .

Notes

1   E.M. Forster, 'George Crabbe: The Poet and the Man', *Listener*, May 29, 1941.

2   Serge Koussevitzky (1874-1951), Russian conductor, patron of contemporary music and the Director of the Boston Symphony Orchestra.

3   See Philip Brett's analysis of the scenario and libretto material preserved in the Britten-Pears Library, in *Peter Grimes*, Cambridge Opera Handbooks (1983). pp. 47-87.

4   Britten and Isherwood had worked together for the Group Theatre in London during the 1930s. Britten composed the incidental music for the Group Theatre's productions of the Auden-Isherwood plays *The Ascent of F6* (1937) and *On the Frontier* (1938). Isherwood, together with W.H. Auden, emigrated to North America in 1939 and has since then been resident in California.

5   Lawrance Collingwood (1887-1982), Principal Conductor of opera at Sadler's Wells from 1931 and Musical Director of Sadler's Wells Opera from 1941 to 1947.

6   Herbert Menges (1902-1972), then Assistant Conductor of Sadler's Wells Opera.

7   Sir Tyrone Guthrie (1900-1971), General Administrator of the Old Vic and Sadler's Wells Companies.

8   Boosey & Hawkes were Britten's publishers from 1936 to 1963.

9   Ralph Hawkes (1898-1950), chairman of Boosey & Hawkes and the man responsible for taking Britten on to the catalogue.

10 Eric Crozier (b. 1914) went on to become a founder Artistic Director of the EOG and the Aldeburgh Festival. He wrote the texts of *Albert Herring, St Nicolas, Let's Make an Opera* (*The Little Sweep*) and, with E.M. Forster, *Billy Budd*.

11 Reginald Goodall (b. 1900), conductor.

12 Kenneth Green (b. 1916) was himself from East Anglia.

13 *Gloriana* was first performed at a Royal Gala at Covent Garden on June 8, 1953.

14 Joan Cross, Norman Del Mar and I took part in an open discussion on *Gloriana* for the Camden Festival at the Holborn Library on March 10, 1983. According to Joan Cross, 'Some of the audience who had been at the first performances insisted that there was no sense of failure at all, and that *Gloriana* had been appreciated in the best way possible.'

15 Britten had conducted the original première of *Billy Budd*, on December 1, 1951.

16 Viola Tunnard (1916-1974), accompanist and member of the EOG.

17 According to the *Listener*, 1953, 'Joan Cross gave the dramatic performance of her career, a wonderful impersonation of the great Queen, domineering, capricious, even spiteful, but a woman with charm and an obvious genius for government.'

18 This refers to the melodrama at the end of *Gloriana*, where the Queen is approaching death. In the *Sadler's Wells Magazine* (autumn 1966) Britten recalled that 'the end of *Gloriana* gave William Plomer and me a great deal of trouble — we wanted to focus very much on the Queen in a different way from before and we wanted to do something quite fresh with the time element.'

19 Britten and Plomer revised the final scene for the Sadler's Wells revival in 1966.

20 Basil Coleman (b. 1916), an Artistic Director of the EOG and producer of *Gloriana*.

21 The Earl of Harewood and his first wife, Marion (née Stein), now Mrs Jeremy Thorpe.

22 Lord Harewood secured approval of an opera based on Lytton Strachey's *Elizabeth and Essex* in April 1952. On May 28, *The Times* announced that the Queen had graciously accepted the dedication of an opera to be composed by Britten in honour of her Coronation. See *The Tongs and the Bones*, the memoirs of Lord Harewood, Weidenfeld and Nicolson, 1981, pp. 134-38.

Some Reflections on the Operas of Benjamin Britten

Buxton Orr

'Will you step into the box.' I still remember, on first hearing the deceptively simple string chords that accompany Peter Grimes's emergence from the crowd, the spine-tingling conviction that I was in the presence of a masterpiece. That was at one of the first performances back in 1945, and the impression was confirmed by what immediately followed: the taking of the Oath. The rough interruption by the 'crowner' of each phrase, before Grimes has finished, brass against strings, Ab harmonisation of the reciting note C against D7 harmonisation of the same note, was something more than colourful mood painting: the dramatic situation had found its perfect parallel in musical thought. Other things also struck me — the first words sung had been 'Peter Grimes', called by the court usher, yet the purely instrumental opening of the opera had already announced the name in a phrase soon to be sung to the words 'Peter Grimes, I here advise you!'

It was, I think, that underrated wit of the nineteenth century, Schopenhauer, the only major philosopher really to understand music, who said it was a mere accident of anatomy that in man both speech and music emerged from the same orifice. He was drawing our attention to the fact that, despite apparent evidence to the contrary, conceptual thought and musical thought are profoundly different. Most composers write songs and many write operas, but it takes the special genius of a composer like Britten to achieve the fusion of musical and conceptual thinking that we find in his vocal settings, above all in the operas.

To pursue my examples, think of the compassionate voices of Ellen and Balstrode as, in strict contrary motion, they sing 'We shall be there with him' to the musical shape with which the persecuting crowd has gleefully observed 'Grimes is at his exercise'. Simultaneously to connect and oppose contrasted meanings of the same musical idea is one of the things musical thinking of this quality can do.

These are examples of musical discourse at what one might call *local* level. But what seems to me the unique contribution of Britten to the history and development of the language of opera is his ability to find a *total* musical design to express the dramatic and poetic requirements peculiar to each of his many works in the genre.

It is well known that, as a student, Britten wanted to study with Alban Berg. Parental and official (Royal College) disapproval intervened, and in the end Britten admitted the advantage of having to 'clamber over the wall' instead of being handed the key. He knew *Wozzeck* well, and it is fascinating to hear in that opera flashes of orchestral timbre that have been seized upon and almost unrecognisably expanded in the pages of *Grimes*. But more obvious is the way Britten has taken the idea of many scenes linked by musico-dramatically significant interludes, developing it in his own way. Torn from their legitimate context, like Tovey's famous 'bleeding chunks of meat' from Wagner, the *Four Sea Interludes* are perhaps too well known in the concert hall and must be firmly returned to their place in the opera. Less often heard out of context is the Interlude (IV) in which the previously mentioned phrase 'Grimes is at his exercise' serves as the ever-repeated ground bass of the extended Passacaglia which, whilst linking the two scenes of Act Two, tells musically of the crowd approaching Grimes's hut, thus causing the scramble down the cliff and precipitating the tragedy. The way in which this is more than mere description touches profoundly on the nature of musical thought.

It is, however, in *The Turn of the Screw* (1954) that the idea of linking interludes receives it most obvious and formalised expression. Myfanwy Piper shaped the Henry James story into sixteen scenes, each dealing with one crucial stage in the development of the drama — 'The Journey', 'The Welcome', 'The Letter', and so on — till the tragic culmination of the story in 'The Piano', 'Flora', and finally, 'Miles'. The Prologue with its deliberately florid, stylised delivery gives way to the bare statement of a Theme, a pulse beat before we hear 'I will', the report of the words which are to entrap the Governess in the drama which is to follow. The Theme takes the form of a pattern of the twelve notes of the chromatic scale, not like a Schoenbergian tone-row, nor destined to be used like one, but used as a passacaglia-like Theme symbolising in its rotating contour the gradual turning of the screw as the drama develops. It is in the final scene that this idea is most overtly exposed, as the persistent questioning of Miles reaches its climax, but meanwhile, in the main body of the work, the sixteen scenes are separated by a series of variations on the theme which binds the many disparate and strongly contrasted incidents into a coherent unity.

One other aspect of the musical design should be mentioned here, if only parenthetically. The pattern of keys through which the various scenes and variation/interludes pass is a carefully planned exploration of the twelve possible key-centres. This is not, of course, a peculiarity of Britten's music alone. Yet it is only in the music of Stravinsky and Shostakovich that, in the middle of the twentieth century, a comparable body of work is to be found fruitfully developing the once supposedly outdated structural possibilities of tonality. Some may protest that this is stuff for the musicologists and musical journals, but I would argue that awareness of such factors plays a much larger part in the musical experience of the technically untutored than is generally recognised. That the technical language of the tutored does little to bridge the gap between the experience of music and the understanding of its purely musical nature is another matter. The point of my digression is to encourage those who respond intuitively to music to trust their instincts when technical matters are raised which seem beyond their ken. At the level of purely musical response I would say that they are not.

In *A Midsummer Night's Dream* (1960) a quite different approach is made to the musical design, again with peculiar appropriateness to the needs of the drama. In collaboration with Peter Pears the composer subtly rearranged the unfolding of the story in order to present with maximum clarity the different groupings of the characters. This is reflected in the music by, for example, the magical timbres associated with Tytania and her entourage coloured by boys' voices, Oberon's counter-tenor and the brilliant trumpet arpeggios associated with Puck. The lovers share a characteristic string of notes belonging to the words 'the course of true love never did run smooth', each couple accompanied by their own distinctive rhythm. The Rude Mechanicals can always be heard before they are seen in the sound of a spiky mid-register solo trombone.

To unite these diverse characterisations, Britten has found a separate solution for each of the three Acts. In Act One string tremolos, joined by sliding glissandos, open and close the Act as well as separate the exits and entrances of the various groups of characters; this sound seems to embody the primeval spirit of the Wood which broods over the whole of this Act. In Act Two a sequence of four chords is split into timbres of strings, muted brass, woodwind and high harps and percussion. These chords are treated in various ways and with their twelve-note content (again quite un-Schoenbergian in its deployment) permeate and unite the events of this Act in the notion of sleep. It is worth mentioning that so interrelated are Britten's musical and extra-musical thoughts that essentially the same chords, though in a different order, form the basis of a setting of Keats's *Sonnet to Sleep* in the *Serenade* written seventeen years previously. Donald Mitchell was the first to spot this, and I believe Britten himself was unaware of the connection until it was drawn to his attention. In Act Three yet another distinctive musical idea serves to frame the awakening of the groups of characters into the clarity and transfiguration of morning; high, clear string lines of a pure, diatonic quality interweave, far in sound and meaning from the sliding obscurity of the strings in Act One.

Britten's musical wit is not often a subject for comment (the bitter and satirical face of this went largely unrecognised in misunderstandings of the television opera *Owen Wingrave*, 1971). The Pyramus and Thisbe scene demonstrates his clear, uncomplicated sense of humour. It provides the usual opportunities for the superimposition of producers' jokes, but the humour is already in the music, not only in the operatic pastiches but supremely in the games with mismanaged word-setting such as might be perpetrated by far less excusable exponents than Peter Quince and Co.. I have often thought that this part of the work could almost be detached and sent into the world entitled 'How Not to Make an Opera'.

Everyone is said to be able to remember exactly what they were doing when they learned of the assassination of President Kennedy. I had just come out of a concert performance of *Gloriana* given as a fiftieth birthday present to the composer at the Royal Festival Hall. Britten had characteristically referred to *Gloriana*, in his short speech of thanks, as 'this old piece', but his hurt at its early unfavourable reception was evident. Its première had been aptly epitomised in *Punch* by a mock review which described at length the Royal occasion itself as 'Act One' followed by a brief resumé of the plot of the first act under the title 'First Interval'. Fortunately the quality of the work has now been recognised and it is back in its legitimate place in the opera house.

The special feature of the musical design of *Gloriana* is its ability to take into the dramatic shape the festive events through which the story threads. Act One opens with the off-stage joust, followed by the trumpet-heralded appearance of Elizabeth. Act Two contains the Choral Dances on the Royal Progress through Norwich, and the Court Dances during which the Queen makes the fateful decision to send Essex to Ireland. It is, however, the end of the opera which employs the most striking musico-dramatic idea. I confess that, to me, as to many others, this had at first caused some misgivings. It was eventually the cover design for the vocal score that gave me the clue. John Piper's costume design for the Queen is depicted there, but it lacks the presence of its wearer: a perfect symbol, it seems to me now, for the end of the opera. As the figure of the Queen fades from our view, so does the sound of her people and their idealising, myth-making anthem, 'Green leaves are we, red rose our golden Queen'. This sweet music is false comfort, ironically juxtaposed as it is with the spoken texts from the real Elizabeth I and the impassioned full orchestral music that punctuates them. I cannot have been alone in taking more than one hearing to recognise, in this dramatically insistent music, a literal quotation of the gentle and moving Second Lute Song, that Essex had sung to Elizabeth in Act One. Once the connection is recognised, the ending achieves its full musico-dramatic impact. Side by side

73

The opening scene of 'Gloriana', designed by John Piper, at Covent Garden in 1953 (photo: Roger Wood)

with the Historical Figure one hears in the music the pain of the human sacrifice that has been made.

There is no more extreme example to support my claim of Britten's ability to reconcile the irreconcilable, musical thought and conceptual thought. Perhaps the very effort I had to make to grasp his achievement could be used as an argument against such a claim. So therefore let me end with an example about which I never had any doubt and one for which, perhaps significantly, I can offer no easy verbal explanation.

In *Curlew River* (1964), operatic but not of the opera house (with a libretto also by William Plomer), the almost painfully slow progress of the story to the moment at which the spirit of the dead boy appears would be difficult to accept outside the tradition of the Noh plays on which it is based. And certainly the almost immediate folding up of the trappings of performance after that crucial event would seem an anti-climax in any convention. Yet such is the power of Britten's musical design that one experiences a sense of inevitability leading to that brief moment of baffling simplicity after which nothing more need be said. The performers leave — almost steal away — with the music with which they had earlier entered the performing area, leaving us in a state of transfixed musical, and spiritual, satisfaction.

I have felt such overwhelmingly simple musical design, and I do mean 'musical', in only one other dramatic context. My experience of *Waiting for Godot*, that of a two part design whose second act is a musically developed repetition of the first, preceded — and still dominates — any purely verbal explanation I can make of that play; elsewhere in Beckett I have had comparable 'musical' experiences.

The provocative comment of Schopenhauer, which I have tried to expand, alerted us to the danger of thinking one thing in terms of another. I doubt if I could demonstrate how I find Beckett's plays to be music, as distinct from the way in which they clearly deal with concepts about which one can talk. But the purely musical coherence of Britten's operas is so subtly related to the conceptual ideas they contain that there is surely a sense in which they lead us into an area of artistic truth that is beyond the category of either words or music.

74

'A daring experiment'
An introduction to *Elizabeth and Essex*

Michael Holroyd

One evening in March 1952 at the Austrian ski-ing resort of Gargellen, three men and a woman sat gossiping about music. What was national expression in opera? What were the national operas of different countries? Did England have a national equivalent of *Aida, The Bartered Bride, Boris Godunov?* The four people were Benjamin Britten, Peter Pears, the Earl of Harewood and his first wife, Marion. And the consensus of their opinions was that England did not have such an opera: in which case, Lord Harewood suggested to Britten, 'you had better write one'.

The previous month King George VI had died, leaving his elder daughter Elizabeth to succeed him. So the most appropriate choice of subject naturally struck them as Elizabeth I. By the time they went to bed several hours later, their schemes were far-advanced. Britten would compose a new opera that would be performed as part of the Coronation celebrations next year. The libretto was to be written by the poet and novelist William Plomer and based on Lytton Strachey's *Elizabeth and Essex* which Lord Harewood had recently been reading.

As soon as he returned to London Lord Harewood began converting these late-night plans into reality. He divided the book into operatic scenes and approached Plomer who agreed to write the libretto. Lytton Strachey had been dead for over twenty years, but Plomer vividly recalled meeting him in the late 1920s, shortly after coming (via Japan) from his home in South Africa to live in England. 'Strachey was then still in his forties, but his beard and spectacles made him look older', Plomer wrote in his autobiography.

> . . . About Strachey's eyelids, as he looked out through the windows of his spectacles over the quickset hedge of his beard, there was a suggestion of world-weariness: he had in fact just two more years to live. I did not think of him in terms of a sum of years but as an intelligence alert and busy behind the appendage of hair and the glass outworks. A glint came into his eyes, the brain was on the move as swiftly as a bat, and when he spoke it was sometimes in the voice of a bat.

Though Britten and Plomer placed more emphasis than Strachey on Elizabeth's pre-eminence as a Queen, they took full advantage of the dramatic nature of the biography to make the opera a glittering pageant. Some characters — Sir Francis Bacon and Sir John Harrington for example — are omitted; and some dramatic episodes (such as the occasion when Essex turns his back on the Queen and has his ears boxed by her) are merely referred to rather than exploited. But despite such differences the themes of both opera and book, with their ceremonial and psychological scenes, their conflict of public and private interests, old age and youth, are closely connected. Britten's work is a translation into musical terms of the duality of Strachey's writing, displacing one person's concealed autobiography by another's, and using a similar blend of sixteenth- and twentieth-century artistic forms. The controversial largely-spoken epilogue, too, is characteristically Stracheyesque in its recall of past life shortly before death.

Lytton Strachey by Simon Bussy

William Plomer by Edward Wolfe

Strachey's ambivalent treatment of the central relationship between Elizabeth and Essex may have prompted William Plomer to concentrate his libretto on the Queen, allowing the other characters (who could have been fully drawn) to remain as surfaces reflecting her extravagant personality. In the opinion of David Cairns this resulted in Britten's *Gloriana* being 'a genuine historical opera' (*Responses* 1973) as original in conception as Strachey's biography had been. Certainly the dramatic character and structure of *Elizabeth and Essex* help to illuminate the opera.

Strachey had begun his 'tussle with the Virgin Queen' on December 17, 1925, completing the first two pages* that day. None of his biographies was to give him so much trouble. Partly this was a matter of stamina: he was by then in his forty-fifth year and becoming more quickly prone to exhaustion. But there were other reasons: the story intertwined in a complicated way with his own love-life and involved the spending of much emotional energy; also he was attempting in this book an experiment that was to test new techniques in biography.

Most of the writing he did at Ham Spray House, near Hungerford, where he was looked after and watched over by Carrington†; most of the research he pursued in the Reading Room of the British Museum, staying round the corner at 51 Gordon Square, the Strachey family home. 'Nobody can be more disgusted by my delay than myself', he wrote to the publishers Chatto and Windus after his first year's work. 'I am in hopes that I may be able to finish something on Queen Elizabeth before very long — certainly in less than a year — I hope much less . . . but I feel rather doubtful about the whole thing.' Some days this doubt deepened into 'complete despair' and he considered abandoning the book. Then he would take it up again: 'I have written a fair amount, and hope to continue', he reported on June 17, 1927, adding 'a most unpleasant

* The manuscript of *Elizabeth and Essex* is in Duke University, North Carolina.

† Dora de Houghton Carrington (1893-1932), known as Carrington, had been a student at the Slade School of Fine Art. At the end of 1915 she fell in love with Strachey and the two of them, living together, formed the nucleus of an emotionally complex Bloomsbury circle. After Strachey's death Carrington committed suicide.

form of occupation in my opinion — but one simply has to!'

A fair amount, after eighteen months, was twenty-five thousand words — barely a third of the final narrative. Between its author's illnesses, flirtations, and recuperative holidays, *Elizabeth and Essex* 'slowly trundled forwards'. Visitors to Ham Spray would observe him desperately at work on it. 'I feel I must stick to this wretched grindstone, or all will be lost', he apologized. At the beginning of March 1928, he wrote from Ham Spray to Roger Senhouse: 'Here I am all alone — it is wonderfully peaceful — a faint mist hangs about — but so far I have managed to keep it out of my head. The Bess crisis is pretty serious — a regular death-grapple!' This death-grapple persisted for another two months until, on the last day of April, Strachey came out the winner. 'I am glad to be able to tell you', he wrote to his publisher, 'that my book is finished'.

In a letter to his sister Dorothy Bussy, Strachey had complained of having led 'a dog's life, between Queen Elizabeth's love affairs and my own'. It was Maynard Keynes who first detected the interaction between Strachey's life and that of his subjects. 'You seem, on the whole, to imagine yourself as Elizabeth,' Keynes suggested, 'but I see from the pictures that it is Essex whom you have got up as yourself. But I expect you have managed to get the best of both worlds.'

Shortly before beginning *Elizabeth and Essex*, Strachey had met and fallen in love with a good-looking young man 'with a melting smile and dark grey eyes' called Roger Senhouse*. He seems to have sensed a parallel between his feelings for this young man and those of Elizabeth for the Earl of Essex. But, since he tended to fall in love with the kind of person he would have liked to be (blue-eyed rowing blues, muscular mountaineers, young Old Etonians), so, at one remove, Essex became a romanticized version of himself. It was this mingling of his own emotional life with that of his characters that gives a feeling of intimacy to a world that was otherwise remote.

Strachey dedicated *Elizabeth and Essex* to his younger brother and his sister-in-law, James and Alix Strachey, who were then pupils of Sigmund Freud and became his authorized translators into English. The chief psychological influence on *Eminent Victorians* had been Dostoevsky. Lytton did not read German and, until the 1920s (James Strachey's translation of *Group Psychology and the Analysis of the Ego* appeared in 1922) Freud's writings had been available in English only in indifferent versions. By 1926 Lytton had picked up a good deal of Freud from discussions with James and Alix, and come to accept the general premise that unconscious processes, among them infant sexuality and the adult operation of the sex instinct, permeate human thought and action. He avoided technical terms, but used Freudian principles as a method by which to suggest that the 'tragic history' (his subtitle to the book) of Queen Elizabeth and the Earl of Essex was inevitable. In particular, he implemented Freud's theories concerning father-daughter relationships to account for the probable underlying attitude of Elizabeth to Essex's execution. There are a number of passages in the earlier part of the book that prepare us for the description of her sensations on sending Essex to his death where Strachey imagines, rising within her, the spirit of her father who had had his wives executed:

> He would find that she was indeed the daughter of a father who had known how to rule a kingdom and how to punish the perfidy of those he had loved the most. Yes, indeed, she felt her father's spirit within her;

* Roger Henry Pocklington Senhouse (1900-1970), educated at Eton and Magdalen College, Oxford, became a noted book collector, translator from the French, and director of the publishing company Martin Secker & Warburg.

and an extraordinary passion moved the obscure profundities of her being, as she condemned her lover to her mother's death. In all that had happened there was a dark inevitability, a ghastly satisfaction; her father's destiny, by some intimate dispensation, was repeated in hers; it was supremely fitting that Robert Devereux should follow Anne Boleyn to the block. Her father! . . . but in a still remoter depth there were still stranger stirrings. There was a difference as well as a likeness; after all she was no man, but a woman; and was this, perhaps, not a repetition but a revenge? After all the long years of her life-time, and in this appalling consummation, was it her murdered mother who had finally emerged?

How valid are such interpretations? Certainly they make for unorthodox history, and particularly at that time. But after reading the book towards the end of 1928, Freud wrote to Strachey:

> You are aware of what other historians so easily overlook — that it is impossible to understand the past with certainty, because we cannot divine men's motives and the essence of their minds and so cannot interpret their actions . . . with regard to the people of past times we are in the same position as with dreams to which we have been given no associations — and only a layman could expect us to interpret such dreams as those. As a historian, then, you show that you are steeped in the spirit of psycho-analysis. And, with reservations such as these, you have approached one of the most remarkable figures in your country's history, you have known how to track back her character to the impressions of her childhood, you have touched upon her most hidden motives with equal boldness and discretion, and it is very possible that you have succeeded in making a correct reconstruction of what actually occurred.

Strachey had used this Freudian theory of unconscious inevitability as the modern addition to a sixteenth-century mood of superstitious fatalism, and produced a general pattern of predestination: 'There's a divinity that shapes our ends / Rough hew them how we will.'

In retrospect, Strachey seemed destined to write this book. Speaking to Hesketh Pearson in 1921, he had pondered the idea of following his *Queen Victoria* with a Life of Queen Elizabeth; and as early as 1909 he had submitted a blank verse play entitled *Essex: A Tragedy* for a Stratford-upon-Avon drama competition. The action of this play covers chapters XIII to XVI of *Elizabeth and Essex*. The last passage of Chapter XII, portraying Essex's forbidden return from Ireland on September 28, 1599, gives an exact description of the dramatic opening scene of the play, reading in places like the stage and costume directions.

A quarter of an hour later — it was ten o'clock — the Earl was at the gate. He hurried forward, without a second's hesitation; he ran up the stairs, and so — oh! he knew the way well enough — into the presence chamber, and thence into the privy chamber; the Queen's bedroom lay beyond. He was muddy and disordered from his long journey, in rough clothes and riding boots; but he was utterly unaware of any of that, as he burst open the door in front of him. And there, quite close to him, was Elizabeth among her ladies, in a dressing-gown, unpainted, without her wig, her grey hair hanging in wisps about her face, and her eyes starting from her head.

Joan Cross and Peter Pears as Elizabeth and Essex (photo: Roger Wood)

It is as a play, a five-act Elizabethan drama, that Strachey constructed this biography. *Elizabeth and Essex* is his *Antony and Cleopatra*. In one of his reviews for the *Spectator*, published in the same year as the composition of *Essex: A Tragedy*, he had written: 'There is only one thing which could have blinded a man in Antony's position so completely as we now know he actually was blinded, and that thing is passion.' Passion is the over-riding motive in *Elizabeth and Essex*. Essex, whose sensual temperament and genius for friendship are brought out by Strachey in a style that emphasizes this similarity to Antony, leaves and returns to his Queen as Antony leaves and returns to Cleopatra; and like Antony he dies a violent death. Elizabeth is no Cleopatra, but each in her fashion was 'a lass unparallel'd', the Queen of England's infinite variations of temper making a dramatic equivalent to the 'infinite variety' of the Queen of Egypt. In Sir Robert Cecil, the mastermind of the drama (who performs a function similar to that of Baron Stockmar in *Queen Victoria*), there is a close approximation to the calculating Octavius. Shakespeare closes *Antony and Cleopatra* with the triumph of Octavius; Strachey, in the carefully weighed passage with which *Elizabeth and Essex* ends (a neat reversal of the famous restropective last paragraph in *Queen Victoria*), employs another device from the Elizabethan stage, picturing Essex brooding over the destiny of England and the future of his own house. With some qualifications the comparison may be extended. Essex's loyal friends, Sir Christopher Blount, Henry Cuffe, Lord Southampton, and Sir Charles Travers, who shared his shattered fortunes, may be likened to Shakespeare's Eros and Scarus. But Strachey simplifies his characters. Francis Bacon, 'the serpent', is a blacker villain than Enobarbus; and Sir Walter Raleigh, 'the fox', is infinitely more sinister than Lepidus.

Unlike *Queen Victoria*, the story is not compactly gathered round the main regal figure, but carried along in a looser episodic form. The long meditations attributed to the chief characters also have their origin in the monologues of Elizabethan drama. Strachey uses indirect speech so as to present the facts as seen by the characters themselves and to echo their tricks of speech. 'The Attorney-Generalship fell vacant, and Essex immediately declared that

Francis Bacon must have the post', he writes. Then, slipping into Essex's own thoughts and manner, he proceeds: 'He was young and had not yet risen far in his profession — but what of that? He deserved something even greater; the Queen might appoint whom she would, and if Essex had any influence, the right man, for once, should be given preferment.'

Wherever possible, Strachey treats his readers as direct onlookers — that is to say, as an audience. Avoiding any formulated interpretation of action, he endeavours to transform every source — letters, diaries and documentary eyewitness accounts — into pictorial terms.

> Howard was Lord Admiral, but Essex was an Earl; which was the higher? When a joint letter to the Queen was brought for their signature, Essex, snatching up a pen, got in his name at the top, so that Howard was obliged to follow with his underneath. But he bided his time — until his rival's back was turned; then, with a pen-knife, he cut out the offending signature; and in that strange condition the missive reached Elizabeth.

In another instance, Strachey brings in word for word a letter from Essex to Elizabeth in such a way that the reader is given the impression he is watching Essex writing, since Strachey interrupts the text several times: 'as he wrote, he grew warmer', and 'now he could hold himself in no longer', and again 'the whole heat of his indignation was flaring out'. The biographical narrative reads in places like directions for a group of actors. In the scene, for example, where Elizabeth makes her speech to an assembly called by the Speaker of the House of Commons, he uses her exact words and at the same time provides us with instructions as to how they should be delivered: 'There was a pause; and then the high voice rang out', and 'She stopped, and told them to stand up, as she had more to say to them', and 'Pausing again for a moment, she continued in a deeper tone'. Then, at the end of Chapter XVI, he writes: 'She straightened herself with a final effort; her eyes glared; there was a sound of trumpets; and, turning from them in her sweeping draperies — erect and terrible — she walked out'. These great visual scenes are framed by such theatrical entrances and exits. When Essex has just been appointed Lord Deputy of Ireland at a council meeting, Strachey handles the exit in a single sentence: 'With long elated strides and flashing glances he left the room in triumph; and so — with shuffling gait and looks of mild urbanity — did Robert Cecil.'

Queen Victoria and *Elizabeth and Essex* are love stories. Strachey's description of Victoria's strong sexuality and his suggestion that Albert may have been homosexual, were almost tastefully accomplished. But when he moves from the Mother Empress to the Virgin Queen, his tone becomes far more erotic. Probing the secret of Elizabeth's virginity, he writes:

> Though, at the centre of her being, desire had turned to repulsion, it had not vanished altogether; on the contrary, the compensating forces of nature had redoubled its vigour elsewhere. Though the precious citadel itself was never to be violated, there were surrounding territories, there were out-works and bastions over which exciting battles might be fought, and which even, at moments, be allowed to fall into the bold hands of an assailant.

To emphasize the way in which the psychological disturbance of Elizabeth's childhood had made sexual intercourse impossible for her, Strachey invented on the queen's behalf an early traumatic experience. 'Manhood — the fascinating, detestable entity, which had first come upon her concealed in yellow magnificence in her father's lap — manhood was overthrown at last, and in the person of that traitor it should be rooted out. Literally, perhaps . . . she knew well enough the punishment for high treason.'

The punishment for treason included castration to which, throughout the book, there are numerous allusions. 'We are aware', wrote Edmund Wilson, 'for the first time disagreeably of the high-voiced old Bloomsbury gossip gloating over the scandals of the past as he ferreted them out in his library.'

A preoccupation with sexual themes and deviations, even when given the imprimatur of Freud, is irregular among historians, and the book has tended to be under-valued in comparison with its predecessors. It is true that *Elizabeth and Essex* has less wit and fire than *Eminent Victorians*, and that Strachey's research among published works (unlike that for *Queen Victoria*) was incomplete. He manipulated historical data by dovetailing fragments of letters and conversations and by editing speeches without ellipsis. Essex, too, is a character of little historical significance (he finds no place for example in G.M. Trevelyan's *History of England*). In a sense the book is not history at all but, as G.B. Harrison described it, 'a fine scenario'. Even so, some historians have found it useful, Conyers Read seeing here 'some brilliant glimpses of her (Elizabeth) and her court'; J.B. Black describing it as a 'penetrating and suggestive study'; and A.L. Rowse judging it to be a 'brilliant and insufficiently appreciated book'.

As a contribution to the art of biography, though praised by E.M. Forster as being in some ways Strachey's 'greatest work', this book has never been wholly accepted. It occupies among Strachey's non-fiction a place similar to that of *Orlando* among the fiction of Virginia Woolf, who believed that *Elizabeth and Essex* represented a misuse of Strachey's imagination: 'he becomes all purple and gold, like the cheaper effects at the Pantomime'. In her essay 'The Art of Biography', she called it 'a daring experiment, carried out with magnificent skill', which, though it failed through flouting the natural limitations of biography, might lead 'the way to further discoveries'.

Elizabeth Fretwell as Elizabeth and Derek Hammond Stroud as Cecil in the 1966 Sadler's Wells production (photo: Anthony Crickmay)

Scenes from Colin Graham's Sadler's Wells production, designed by Alix Stone: left, Jennifer Vyvyan, 1967 and, right, Anne Evans, 1975 as Lady Rich; below Sylvia Fisher as Elizabeth in the final scene (photos: Zoë Dominic, Donald Southern)

The Librettist of 'Gloriana'

Rupert Hart-Davis

William Plomer was poet, novelist, editor and critic. He was born in South Africa in 1903, of English parents. He was a sickly child and was often taken on the long journey to England for the sake of his health. His first school in Johannesburg was followed by an English preparatory school and Rugby, where he spent most of the Great War.

After the war, back with his family in South Africa, he worked as a trainee farmer in the wild Stormberg Mountains in the Eastern Province. Then he helped his father to run a 'kaffir store' and farm in Zululand. His liking for and admiration of the blacks, which had begun with his first nurse, grew steadily as he got to know more of them, and these feelings persisted for the rest of his life.

Somehow he found time to write his first novel *Turbott Wolfe*. He sent it to Leonard and Virginia Woolf, who published it at their Hogarth Press in 1926. Its savage satire on the cruelties and injustices of South African life caused an outburst of rage throughout that country. As Plomer's friend Roy Campbell wrote in his poem *The Wayzgoose*:

> Plomer, 'twas you who, though a boy in age,
> Awoke a sleepy continent to rage,
> Who dared alone to thrash a craven race
> And hold a mirror to its dirty face.

That same year Campbell and Plomer started a magazine called *Voorslag* (*Whiplash*), and wrote most of it themselves, until they were joined by a young South African journalist called Laurens Van der Post. The magazine caused as much uproar as *Turbott Wolfe*, but lasted only three months.

Van der Post made friends with a remarkable Japanese mariner called Captain Mori, who commanded a ship trading between Japan and South Africa. He invited Van der Post and Plomer to accompany him on the round trip. Van der Post stayed in Japan only as long as the ship was there, but Plomer lived in the country for two years, adopting Japanese ways and earning his living by teaching English in schools and universities, to which he was introduced by his friend the poet Edmund Blunden. As a result of these experiences Plomer published a book of stories (*Paper Houses*, 1929) and a novel (*Sado*, 1931).

In 1929 he returned to England by way of the Trans-Siberian railway, and at first felt very much a displaced person, but he soon, largely through the kindness of the Woolfs, met many of the English intelligentsia. He continued to write and publish poems, novels and short stories. A murder in the London boarding house where he was living gave him the idea for his most successful novel *The Case is Altered* (1932).

In 1937 he succeeded Edward Garnett as principal reader to the publisher Jonathan Cape, and before long he made a discovery that was to bring him perhaps more fame than anything he wrote himself. One day, among the batch of the week's typescripts that awaited him in Cape's office, were two battered notebooks filled with the diary of an unknown curate of the 1870s, tightly written in an angular sloping hand, and a note saying that twenty other such volumes were available. Plomer conscientiously, but without much expectation, took the two notebooks home to read, and a week later reported

83

excitedly that he was much impressed with their quality and was sending for the other twenty. His brilliant edition of *Kilvert's Diary* was published in three volumes in 1938, 1939 and 1940. Later he produced a one-volume selection, which has been in print ever since. Admirers of the diary grew steadily, and a Kilvert Society was formed, in which Plomer played a leading part, attending all its meetings and lecturing on Kilvert and his diary all over the country. The Society still flourishes today.

Plomer spent most of the second world war in the Information Section of Naval Intelligence in the Admiralty, for which his friend Ian Fleming had recommended him. All he was able to write during those years were the first volume of his autobiography (*Double Lives*, 1943) and a number of macabre and extremely funny ballads, for which he later became famous.

After the war he returned to Cape as reader, and was soon able to repay Ian Fleming's kindness by persuading Cape to publish Fleming's first thriller, thus making a great deal of money for everyone except himself.

In 1948 he was invited to lecture on Edward FitzGerald at the first Aldeburgh Festival. Probably the invitation came from Benjamin Britten himself, since the lecture was reprinted in *Tribute to Benjamin Britten on his Fiftieth Birthday* (1963). Be that as it may, the two men became great friends, and when Britten had persuaded E.M. Forster to write him a libretto for his next opera, it was Plomer who suggested as a subject Herman Melville's *Billy Budd*, which became one of Britten's most successful works.

In 1952 the Queen approved the suggestion that Britten should write a Coronation opera on the theme of Elizabeth I and Essex, and Britten asked Plomer to write the libretto for *Gloriana*. Plomer's notes on it will be found on page 99.

In 1955 Britten, planning a journey to the Far East, asked Plomer what he should see in Japan. Plomer strongly recommended the theatre, especially the traditional Noh plays. Britten was much impressed by them and asked Plomer once again to be his librettist. They decided that the only way they could achieve the silent intentness of a Japanese audience was to produce the opera in a church. Thus *Curlew River* (1964) was first performed in the ancient church of Orford in Suffolk, as part of the Aldeburgh Festival, as were its successors, *The Burning Fiery Furnace* (1966) and *The Prodigal Son* (1968), all with librettos by Plomer. Also he took part in every Aldeburgh Festival.

His last twenty years were spent in Sussex, first at Rustington, then at Hassocks, where he died in September 1973, shortly before his seventieth birthday.

Although he was reclusive by nature, refused ever to have a telephone, and liked to keep his address as private as possible, he had innumerable friends in whose company he was gay, witty and endearing. His loyalty and integrity were absolute. In his *Collected Poems* can be found this self-epitaph:

> Sometimes thinking aloud
> He went his own way.
> He was joky by nature,
> Sad, sceptical, proud.
> What he never would follow,
> Or lead, was a crowd.

The Music of 'Gloriana'

Christopher Palmer

Of all that has been written about this most controversial of Britten's operas, the one article which seems to me to strike straight to the heart of the matter is Donald Mitchell's 'Public and Private Life in *Gloriana*' (*Opera*, October 1966, pp 767-774), in which he argues that the opera's central theme is to be found in Elizabeth's aria 'The Queen's Dilemma' (Act Three, scene three). She knows she is expected to sign the death-warrant of the man found guilty of treason, yet with whom she is in love. Will she or won't she? The aria ends 'I am, and am not; freeze, and yet I burn; since from myself my other self I turn'. Here is the crux: the Queen's 'public' self — the one that must rule and govern — bids her destroy the noble Earl of Essex; whereas her other 'private' self — her inner promptings — urges her to save him. All the opera's dramatic development, claims Dr Mitchell, radiates outward from this central antithesis.

This public-private dichotomy is in fact the principal recurrent thematic force in nearly all Britten's operas: that is to say the conflict between the individual and society; between what a man would prefer to do as opposed to what others expect him to do; between emotion and reason, business and pleasure, personal gratification and the common weal, Establishment and anti-Establishment. Peter Grimes wants to be an individualist; as a result he is despised, rejected and finally destroyed by the close-knit society into which he refuses to fit. Albert Herring has one brief alcoholic burst of glory: he defies the puritanical and prurient petty-mindedness of his native village community which refuses to recognise the need for sexual self-expression and 'does up instincts with safety-pins'. Yet whatever wild oats Albert may or may not have sown (Lady Billows: 'the havoc wrought by gin!') he quickly returns (to continue the metaphor) to plough the furrow of convention and submit those erring, assertive 'instincts' to death by slow torture — the torture of abnegation and repression. Lucretia is another sacrificial victim. She chooses to die rather than live with self-knowledge: she cannot accept the existence of an adulterous passion within her breast, the fact that she yielded to Tarquinius because she *wanted* to, not because she was *forced* to (what, one wonders, would have happened if this particular 'Rape' had reached a modern court of law?). She loves her husband and would wish him to be the focal point of her 'private' as well as her 'public' feelings; but Tarquinius breaks in and the house of her life is destroyed. In *Billy Budd* Captain Vere is fatally (for Billy) torn between his attraction to Billy, his (private) awareness of Billy's essential goodness, and the sense of (public) duty which compels him to sentence to death any man guilty of killing a superior officer, even if that officer — Claggart — is the personification of evil. Here in *Budd*, which was composed immediately before *Gloriana*, is a direct anticipation of the latter insofar as Vere's conflict, like Elizabeth's, is not merely between duty and inclination. As Hans Keller has observed*, the Queen objects not only to what is false in Essex's love for her and prompted by self-seeking, but also to the fact that he arouses in her a conflict which she hoped she had resolved: 'when she signs his death-warrant, she proves herself to herself once more — and it is not only her

* *Tempo* Winter, 1966, p. 3

dutiful Queen's self she proves, but also her personal, anti-sexual self, a guilty self of which her duties are, psychologically, a displacement.' Is not the parallel with Vere quite striking? — for there is an undeniable element of suppressed sexuality, of unwelcome and deeply-concealed self-knowledge in his relationship with Billy. Billy awakens a conflict which Vere hoped *he* had resolved; and when *he* signs *Billy's* death-warrant he also 'proves himself to himself', not merely his dutiful Captain's self but his 'personal, anti-sexual self'. There may be no such person-to-person conflict in *Owen Wingrave* but, here again, the hero is publicly expected to conform to family tradition and know no other life but war; he rebels, seeks to act in accordance with his own private pacifist inclinations and instincts — and in so doing signs his own death-warrant as irrevocably as the Queen signs Essex's and Vere Billy's. The most pitiful case

Jennifer Vyvyan (Lady Rich), Geraint Evans (Mountjoy), Peter Pears (Essex) and Monica Sinclair (Lady Essex) at Covent Garden in 1953 (photo: Roger Wood)

of all is that of Aschenbach in *Death in Venice*. Here sex (essentially absent from *Owen Wingrave*) leaps back into disastrous prominence when a public figure of international stature develops a hopeless and demeaning passion for a boy young enough to be his grandson. He is the more susceptible in that he, like Queen Elizabeth, is ageing fast and, in fact, directly *en route* for the grave; (the Queen's death is still some way off and she can salvage some remnant of public dignity through eliminating Essex). But Aschenbach is come face to face with the abyss, he has no power over Tadzio, so nothing remains for him but ruin and degradation. Like both *Budd* and *Gloriana*, *Death in Venice* is a deeply-considered, elaborately-worked variation on the theme of beauty, physical attraction, as a force for evil and disruption.

Gloriana was of course conceived as a 'public' opera in a very special sense inasmuch as it was commissioned to mark the coronation of Queen Elizabeth II, the intention being that the *first* Elizabethan era would be assisting at the birth of what was confidently expected to be the *second*. It was therefore assumed that the opera would present a recognisably 'public' face to the world; which indeed it did (and does). But what it *also* does — and this is doubtless what upset some of the early critics (both musical and non-musical) who were, one assumes, expecting some piece of naive and trumpery jingoism — is to reveal the mind's construction, as it were, behind that fair and splendid face: music being of all the arts the one best equipped to make such revelations both by reason of its penetrative insight, the directness and universality of its expression, and its power of moving dramatically on more than one level simultaneously. *Gloriana* is a case in point; to quote Mitchell (*op. cit.*) again, 'the grand accumulation of pageant, pomp and ceremony . . . is an outward projection of the inner dramatic situation; and therein lies the strength and relevance of the spectacle'.

Photographs by Roger Wood of scenes from the world première of 'Gloriana' at Covent Garden in 1953, designed by John Piper; above, Norwich; below, Whitehall

87

[1] Very lively ♩ = 180

[2] (♩ = 56)

ESSEX

Good Fran - ces,   do not weep
F   C   Gmi

Let us first explore this 'outward projection'. William Plomer, in adapting his libretto from Lytton Strachey's *Elizabeth and Essex*, was much concerned to make the Queen the central character and to portray her as a public figure (a) by showing something of her relationship to her subjects, and (b) by sketching in some characteristic background details of the Elizabethan public scene. The first of these comes in the orchestral prelude which depicts a tournament in progress (Ex. 1) and of which a number of features are worth remarking insofar as they epitomise the stylistic tenets of the opera as a whole: simplicity and accessibility. *Formal* simplicity: bars 5-11 of my Ex. 1 are in essence a rhythmic, rather than a melodic, development of the fanfare in bars 1-4, and the percussion ritornello (one bar of which is shown) leads in an exact formal repetition of the entire segment, but with different (though related) music. The same pattern then goes on repeating itself, with constantly recurring variation of content. This original notion has a childlike simplicity. (The entire opera in fact is constructed as a mosaic of individual units — set-pieces, songs, arias, recitatives and ensembles — rather than as a continuously-evolving symphonic narrative as in *Billy Budd*.) A similar principle of originality-in-simplicity is present in the harmonic sphere, which is consistently diatonic; the common chord or triad is ever to the fore. Bars 1-4 of Ex. 1 are a case in point; so is the lovely quartet in Act Two scene three, ('Good

88

[3] Steady ♩ = 72

QUEEN
Fail not to come to court___ in fine or dir-ty wea-ther,

[4] Quiet and flowing ♩ = 70   always *p*   CECIL
The art of gov-ern-ment Is

in pro-cras-ti-na-tion and In si-lence and de-(lay);

Frances, do not weep') in which Essex, Mountjoy and Penelope Rich try to comfort Lady Essex after she has been humiliated by the Queen (Ex. 2); so too is the Ensemble of Reconciliation at the end of Act One scene one, in which a contrapuntal texture of great richness and beauty issues from a simple song-like tune which is one of Britten's most attractive melodic inventions (Ex. 3). The placing of ordinary common chords at strategic points in Cecil's Song of Government (Act One, scene two) offers a subtle psychological insight (Ex. 4): in the shifty cross-rhythms of bars 1-3 we can see the politician's dexterous manoeuvring, in the F major triad of bar 4 his stealthy pausing to look about him and determine which way the wind is blowing. Sir Walford Davies called triads 'God's chords'; here, then, it is surely a case in musical terms of *vox dei, vox populi*, since Britten's new-old harmonic idiom has always been a major factor in the wide popular appeal of his music.

To return to the start of the opera: the tournament scene itself is composed into (and out of) the music of the Prelude in much the same way as Act One scene one of *Peter Grimes* is built around the music of the immediately preceding First Sea Interlude. (What an invaluable labour-and-money-saving expedient is music! To show the tournament itself would be costly and difficult; and why bother, when *music* can bring it so vividly before the mind's eye?) This tournament scene has a dual function. It is at once spectacle-in-itself and designed to give us an important first insight into Essex's character: impetuous, emotional, inflammable. He hates the thought of Mountjoy the victor finding favour in the Queen's sight and loses no time in goading him (literally, with repeated stabs of a D minor chord) into a fight. The duel-music is athletic and muscular and, as is always the case with Britten's descriptive or action music, devoid of cinémusical cliché. This motif, developed as a fugato, later introduces Act One scene two and, as it were, shadow-boxes away throughout the Queen's dialogue with Cecil in which Essex's fiery instability is the topic under discussion:

The appearance of the Queen and her retinue at the climax of the duel is heralded by a flourish of trumpets which, incidentally, was revived to memorable effect to greet the present-day Queen Elizabeth when she arrived to open the newly-converted Maltings Concert Hall at Snape on June 2 1967.

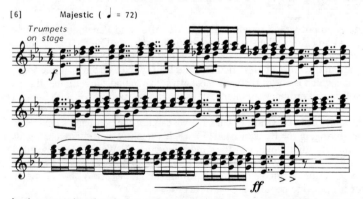

Again we notice the absence of stereotype: the modal harmonic colouring is familiar, less so the melodic and rhythmic substance of the fanfare, which derives more from Purcell than from quasi-military prototypes. Again, the matter of Ex. 6 is not merely decorative, but becomes an integral part of the

Photographs by Zoë Dominic
of the 1966 Sadler's Wells
production, by Colin
Graham, designed by Alix Stone

confrontation scene which follows: its regal sextuplets lend themselves with
remarkable dexterity to a suggestion of fishwives wrangling ('E'en when
fishwives wrangle / They must make an end of words'). At the end of the scene
the royal procession moves off to a splendidly majestic development of Ex. 6 in
the guise of a ceremonial march; and that, alas, is all we are to hear of it. Not so
Ex. 7a, one of the most important themes of the opera:

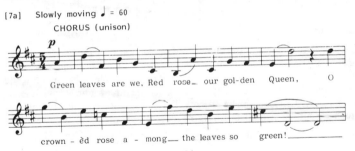

91

This represents another facet of Elizabeth's public image: her warm and loving relationship with her subjects. Its gracefully-inclining sixths and no less gracefully-rising minor sevenths may suggest the act of bowing in homage; alternatively Eric Walter White's happy notion is that these slowly, smoothly-moving intervals 'unfold like the petals of a cinquefoil Tudor rose'*, the measured overlapping of the vocal parts within a 5/4 rhythm enhancing the impression. This homage-hymn recurs in many contexts throughout the opera, its well-defined melodic shape rendering it instantly recognisable. Yet what a contrast between the essentially feminine graciousness, almost voluptuousness, of Ex. 7a and the masculine assertiveness of Ex. 7b (unison trombones: no less feminine sonority exists in the orchestra) which comes from the last scene in Act One:

For here Elizabeth is acknowledging her willingness to bear her burden, the sceptre and the glory, whatever the cost in human terms may be. (She concludes with a plainchant-like prayer for divine support in which Britten's orchestration contrives the semblance of a myriad murmuring voices and organ in a vast resonant acoustic.) Perhaps the most moving featured use of Ex. 7a is as an *envoi* at the very end of the opera when it is sung off-stage through a protracted diminuendo, the voices moving ever downward and making their exit one by one, like withered petals falling to the ground.

Further light is shed on the Queen as a public figure by the two 'historical' tableaux of Act Two: the one set in Norwich (Act Two scene one) where the Queen is on 'progress' and the citizens perform a masque in her honour, the other a court-ball in the Palace of Whitehall (scene three). The Norwich scene (one can sense Britten's spirits lifting at the thought of being able to draw his native East Anglia into the opera) is preceded by a short orchestral prelude in

* *Benjamin Britten: his life and operas* (new edition, Faber & Faber 1983, p. 198)

which Britten suggests, in exhilarating *alfresco* manner, the huzzahs of the crowd and a clamorous peal of bells (Ex. 8). The unaccompanied Choral Dances featured in the masque ('Time', 'Concord', 'Time and Concord', 'Country Girls', 'Rustics and Fishermen', 'Final Dance of Homage') have won considerable popularity in their own right, and this concept of a choral 'entertainment' recurs in a quite different context in the pentathlon scene in *Death in Venice* where the boys compete in a variety of sports, the style of each being described by the chorus. If no particular 'period' models are invoked in the Choral Dances (once nicely described by Andrew Porter as 'flowers fresh sprung from an English field'), references to Elizabethan music are predictably more plentiful in the Courtly Dances: the Pavane, Galliard, Lavolta, Morris Dance, March and Coranto; although Britten asked Imogen Holst, who was working for him at the time, to be sure to alert him if the music ever started to turn into pastiche*. We see Britten here as a *commentator* rather than a pasticheur, refracting selected formal and linguistic elements of the Elizabethan idiom at his own contemporary angle of vision — or, to put it another way, viewing Elizabeth I from the vantage-point of Elizabeth II. Here, too, Britten shows his skill as a dramatist by placing *private* drama within the framework of *public* ritual. When the Queen suddenly returns hideously bedizened in Lady Essex's missing dress, it prompts the tuba, in its fat and ugly upper register, to a parody of the Lavolta; later the trombone joins in with spitting, paw-swiping *glissandi* that sound suspiciously like miaows. At the end of the scene the wind-band† on stage proceeds with the 'Coranto'; but, as the Court's excited reaction to Essex's new appointment as Lord Deputy in Ireland begins to register, it faces increasingly strenuous competition from, and is eventually rendered inaudible by, the regular orchestra whose assertively strident fourths recall the conspiratorial quartet from the end of the previous scene (Ex. 9)§ and point to trouble in the offing. Which duly arises, for after failing in Ireland, Essex makes a half-hearted attempt to lead a revolt against the Crown. This we learn about in the Ballad-Rondo at the outset of Act Three, which constitutes the last 'public' music in the score. Here we are back in the world of Beaumont and Fletcher's London as portrayed by Britten in the finale of the *Spring Symphony*, complete with raucously chanting ragamuffins; while the gittern-accompanied ballad itself, like Raleigh's 'waggishly sententious' (Peter Evans) song in Act One scene one, clearly relates to Britten's own version of *The Beggar's Opera*, made in 1947-8.

Most of the 'private' music in *Gloriana* is, naturally, concerned with the relationship between Elizabeth and Essex. We should not, however, be misled into assuming that this is exclusively what the opera is 'about'. As the title implies, the chief character in *Gloriana* is the Queen herself, and the opera is a study or portrait rather than a story; there is no real plot or fast-moving sequence of events. Essex exposes the vulnerable feminine side of her nature — remember that she is an ageing woman and he an attractive young man — and, at the same time, reveals that his own motives in bestowing such

* For a fascinating glimpse of Britten at work on the score of *Gloriana*, see Imogen Holst, 'Working for Britten', *Musical Times*, Feb 1977, pp 202-4

† For the *Gloriana* Symphonic Suite Britten re-orchestrated these dances for normal symphony orchestra, the 'Galliard' undergoing a particularly winsome transformation in terms of solo string quartet and *tutti* string orchestra.

§ Something of a real-life parallel to this situation occurred on November 22, 1963 when, during a concert performance of *Gloriana* at the Royal Festival Hall, news of the Kennedy assassination began to seep through the auditorium and gradually, of course, to gain total precedence over the 'stage entertainment'.

[10]

[11]

ESSEX

Queen _____ of my Life!

[12] Quick and gay

ESSEX

Quick mu___ - sic is best When the

Harp

heart, _____ the heart is op - pressed, _____

[13] Very freely (slow) ♩ = about 40

ESSEX

Hap - py, _____ hap _____ - py were

he could fin - ish forth his fate

attentiveness on her are not unmixed. Before Essex's entrance we find the Queen heavily oppressed by cares of state — a slow treadmill-like motif of whole-tone steps, Ex. 10 (the whole-tone scale, being deprived of the normal cadential points of repose, goes on forever; it has neither beginning nor end, and is thus a fitting symbol for the endless demands made on the Queen as a ruler). It is perhaps significant also that this motif is generally given to the woodwinds, a colour frequently associated in Britten with plague and pestilence (the rats in *Our Hunting Fathers*, the Asiatic cholera in *Death in Venice*). Essex's somewhat conventionally impassioned salutation (Ex. 11) fails to banish care from her mind; so does the first, light-hearted lute-song (Ex. 12), through which the persistently dissonant pedal-points (as in the bass of Ex. 12) indicate that she is still oppressed by cares of state. Far more in tune with their melancholic disposition is the C minor of 'Happy we', the most famous number of *Gloriana* (Ex. 13). The first phrase is a quotation from John Wilbye's 1609 madrigal 'Happy, O happy he', but thereafter Britten (as in the Courtly Dances) recreates the emotional *spirit* of Dowland rather than the literal musical *letter* — shades here both of his *Lachrymae* for viola and piano or orchestra, and of the later *Nocturnal* for solo guitar (both after Dowland). The C minor lifts into major for a blithe-sounding central section — what *should* be perhaps *will* be — but then the major sinks back into the minor (always a symbol in Britten's music for the worm within the rose) and we realise that *this* dream has no hope of turning into reality. Certainly not with one so moved to vitriolic outburst as Essex, when he catches sight of Raleigh's silhouette through a thin curtain:

The seconds for muted brass and oboe actually do have a viciously jabbing, pecking sound and movement, and they alight on the low horn chord in bar 5 much as a bird of prey might pounce. This chord (significantly akin to the 'storm' chord in *Peter Grimes* Act One scene one) assumes some later importance in the marvellous music of hurriedly whispered conversation and running footsteps which begins Act Three, and is clearly connected with Essex's failure to crush the rebellion in Ireland and his consequent doom:

[15]   Quick and agitated ♩ = 90

What a contrast musically now, when he bursts in on the Queen in the early morning, she all wigless and un-made-up, greasy with sleep, he conscious of having failed miserably in his mission! Ex. 11 is now quite crestfallen, robbed of all its youthful ardour; even the larks outside are faint of heart ('Because you're here / When larks alone have right of audience'); and the C minor of the lute-song now becomes a leaden-footed funeral march ('Happy *were* we'). After this, the Dressing Table Song is needfully cool and balsamic, with that special tenderness and transparency of texture always characteristic of Britten's writing for concerted female voices, as for instance in the last-act trio when Penelope Rich and Lady Essex (and Mountjoy) come to plead with the Queen for Essex's life ('Great Queen, your champion in a prison cell lies languishing'). The spinning-wheel song in *Lucretia* is another celebrated instance, likewise the quartet for Ellen, Auntie and the two Nieces in *Peter Grimes*.

The lute song's ultimate destiny is, however, even further removed from its original simplicity. The court has found Essex guilty and condemned him in an extraordinary lugubrious trombone pronouncement:

[16]   Very slow ♪ = 72

In the final scene the Queen, having committed her lover to the executioner's block, is left alone in full cognizance of her own mortality, time and place becoming ever less important to her; for she knows full well that in destroying Essex she is destroying a part of herself. This climactic moment is treated melodramatically in the strict sense, i.e. as a combination of spoken words (the real Elizabeth's own) and music — but what music! The tender, wistful lute song, so delicately and fastidiously scored, is now inflated to phantasmagorical proportions, *fortissimo* and weighted down with a monstrously inappropriate full-orchestral apparatus (one recalls Cotten's 'Pastoral', set by Britten in the *Serenade*, in which, when the sun sets and shadows grow long, brambles look like tall cedars, molehills like mountains, ants like elephants). It is a masterstroke: as stark and uncompromising a musical statement as can be

Ryland Davies as Essex beside Sylvia Fisher (Elizabeth) (photo: Reg Wilson)

imagined of the 'theme' (in the widest sense) of the opera. The Queen is adamant in her resolution to put the conscientious discharge of her duties before personal happiness; of the cost to her as a woman this music tells us only too plainly.

At first glance we might suppose that, thematically speaking, *Gloriana* stands apart from Britten's other operas insofar as there is, or appears to be, no corruption of innocence, no betrayal of the young and defenceless. Yet in a sense anyone whose private life is thwarted or rendered virtually non-existent by 'cares of state' (literal or metaphorical) is a corrupted and betrayed innocent, a victim of the curse of consciousness, Hardy's 'disease of feeling' which he, like Britten, so bitterly resented. In a primal paradise such as that into which the child is born there is no schism between pleasure and duty, since the latter is an invention of civilisation. The innocent, the 'natural' man, is (or would be, if he existed) oblivious of the need to do anything but that which seems natural. He is blissfully unaware that, from this point of view, the whole fabric of our life-style is sunk beyond all thinking in the grossest absurdity: that men are forced to spend their lives in activities they were never 'meant' to be engaged in, pursuing aims they were never 'meant' to pursue. Of this Britten was painfully conscious, and as both a public figure and a member of the still oppressed homosexual minority (and let us not forget that for most of his lifetime homosexuality was still a criminal offence) knew that a compromise between public esteem and personal fulfilment is neither easily won nor lightly maintained. It was a question which much preoccupied him, as his music makes manifest; it is likely that he saw both Elizabeth *and* Essex (in whose character the combination of child-like vitality and poetic sensibility would certainly have appealed) as sacrificial victims, both caught inextricably in the net of circumstance and the warring and equivocal impulses of their characters. Both yearn (in the Lute Song) for something which is not theirs; yet would they really want it even if it were? Its very

97

inaccessibility may be part of its attractiveness. To what extent, we wonder, are they fulfilled in being *un*-fulfilled? It is a measure of Britten's integrity and skill that having accepted a commission of an ostensibly 'occasional' nature, he not only met the terms of his contract — admirably — but so widened them as to treat of matters that were of central importance to him both as man and artist. This surely is part of Britten's greatness: that he took opera further out of the sphere of mere mindless entertainment and made of it as broad an arena of human experience as his music could meaningfully accommodate.

Ava June as Elizabeth, a role she sang in the 1972 revival of the Sadler's Wells production and on several European tours (photo: Donald Southern)

Sylvia Fisher as Elizabeth in Lady Essex's finery, Sadler's Wells, (photo: Zoë Dominic)

Notes on the Libretto of 'Gloriana'

William Plomer

Lytton Strachey's *Elizabeth and Essex* is not a book which has pleased everybody, but it was the starting-point of this opera. This is not the place to analyse the book's deficiencies, real or alleged, but to assert that it tells skilfully a tense and dramatic story based upon historical persons and happenings. The late Sir Desmond MacCarthy, in his recently published *Memories*, recalls an interesting opinion that *Elizabeth and Essex* is almost a sketch for a play and that Strachey's method was inspired by or borrowed from the Elizabethan stage. Both the composer and the librettist of *Gloriana* were able to see in the book a sketch for an opera, and both are ready to acknowledge their debt to Strachey's dramatic sense. This does not mean that *Gloriana* is wholly based upon *Elizabeth and Essex*, or that it has emerged merely as an operatic version of that book. In the first place the makers of an opera are not under the obligation of even a picturesque biographer like Strachey to stick closely to history or chronology. Secondly, the makers of this particular opera came to be less concerned than Strachey with the amatory motives of the two principal characters and more concerned with the Queen's pre-eminence as a Queen, a woman, and a personality.

It might be said that Queen Elizabeth I is not only a great figure in European history but in English folklore. Her legendary fame is part of our racial memory, part of every educated or part-educated Englishman's conception of our national character and destiny: therefore to dramatize her life, or any part of it, seems more an act of recollection or evocation than of creation. And what is true of the Queen is to some extent true of the Elizabethan age in general. This does not mean that the composer and librettist simple relied upon Strachey for facts and opinions. They made it their business to extend their understanding of Queen Elizabeth, and of Essex, and of the Elizabethan age, as far as possible, in every relevant direction, beyond its former limits, taking Professor J.E. Neale's authoritative biography as a standard and guide, and going back wherever possible to original sources in art as well as in literature.

Reduced to the barest outline, the theme of the opera may be stated as follows. Queen Elizabeth, a solitary and ageing monarch, undiminished in majesty, power, statesmanship, and understanding, sees in an outstanding young nobleman a hope for both the future of her country and of herself. Essex, young, handsome, bold, of the highest nobility and rank, is perceived by her to be potentially a worthy successor to Leicester and Burleigh, a possible right-hand man or prime minister, who, under her supreme authority and guidance, may in time control and direct the government of England. Essex, for his part, perceives that if he wins the confidence of his ageing sovereign and kinswoman, there may be almost no limit to the power attainable by him. Two human weaknesses make this situation dangerous. They were very well expressed by Sir Robert Naunton in his *Fragmenta Regalia*. The Queen, taken by Essex's nobility, his 'most goodly Person', and his 'kind of urbanity or innate courtesie', conceives a 'violent indulgencie' towards him, which, of its nature, implies the risk of 'non-perpetuity'. Essex, for his part, 'drew in too fast, like a childe sucking on an over-uberous Nurse'; he was 'too bold an ingrosser both of fame and favour', and what he might have managed by tact, and prudence, and patience, he lost by 'an over-desire and thirstiness after fame'. The Queen, who had been ready to make him, was in the end obliged to break him — a tragedy for both. Loyalty at the court of Elizabeth the First tended to express itself in the language of a lover-like devotion, and in responding to the 'violent indulgencie' of the Queen, in 'playing up' to her, Essex may, in spite of the disparity of their ages, have been half carried away in an illusion of lover-like feelings. An ambiguity in the Queen's feelings towards him may have evoked a response in him. Both were complex characters: the Queen had to subdue her inclinations as a woman to her magnificent conception of her position and her duty as a monarch; Essex, a bold man of action, had an imaginative, moody, melancholy bent.

The liberties that have been taken with chronology and other matters are justified, it is hoped, by the demands of opera and of this particular opera, demands for simplification and concentration. Bacon, Shakespeare, Leicester, the Armada, the Queen's speech at Tilbury, for example, have been set aside, which would have been impossible in any historical conspectus of her reign, or in any chronicle-play or pageant-play. The librettist felt that his business was to afford scope for the musical development of the dramatic central theme.

The libretto is partly in verse and partly in prose. The verse is mostly irregular, with an intermittent use of rhyme. In general the lines have been kept short, often with only two or three stresses, and the language fairly direct and colloquial, in order to sustain a brisk dramatic interchange between the characters. The lines tend to grow longer at moments of soliloquy, prayer, or meditation. Bearing in mind always the paramount requirements of the music, the librettist aimed at giving the words such flexibility, such metrical or rhythmical variations, as seemed fitting to each moment, or situation, or new development. Dramatic unity was the general aim, not metrical uniformity.

From the first the question arose to what extent the language was to be genuine or fake Elizabethan. The best answer seemed that it should be neither. The important things were, first, that it should be operatically suitable — and settable — and, more precisely, settable by Britten; next, that it should have an Elizabethan flavour, so long as this was not procured by any self-conscious 'period' seasonings. It seemed advisable to shun anything that might smack of Wardour Street, Merrie England, Good Queen Bess, or the half-baked half-timbering of debased twentieth-century 'Tudor' stylings.

There seemed no need to be afraid of archaisms; of writing *weareth* or *supersedeth* instead of 'wears' or 'supersedes' (these old endings being pleasing to the ear and useful to the composer) or of using words like *plainings*, *ensamples*, *complots*, or *flaskets*. Such words rose up easily from the recesses of the librettist's unconscious memory, and seemed to him, in their settings and his more sanguine moments, to be *mots justes*. No fine combing of the libretto would be necessary to find anachronisms: the use of words of a later than Elizabethan familiarity has been deliberate.

Simple punning or playing upon words was an Elizabethan as well as a later habit. Examples occur in the libretto with the name of Mountjoy in the opening scene, or with Time and Concord in Act Two, scene one. To echo now and then the Elizabethan love of antithesis has not been to aim at Euphuism or turgidity. Examples are a phrase like 'the double image of our single bliss' in Act Two, scene two, or, in the same scene:

> I with the power of love,
> You with the love of power . . .

The recurrent tune associated with the Queen:

> Green leaves are we,
> Red rose our Queen,
> O crownèd rose among the leaves so green!

is derived from the following four lines, written by an Elizabethan boy in one of his school-books:

> The rose is red,
> The leaves are green,
> Long live Elizabeth,
> Our noble Queen.

There is something ancient and persistent and folklorish here: the librettist has lately seen an Early Victorian sampler, worked by a young girl, carrying a plainer intimation of mortality:

> The leaves are green,
> The rose is red,
> This will be seen
> When I am dead.

The occasional ejaculations in Latin put into the mouth of the Queen in the opera were Elizabeth the First's own. She was a superb exponent of plain and memorable English, and a good many of her phrases have been worked into the libretto, some well known, some little known. The prayer at the end of Act One, scene two, is a conflation and adaptation of passages from prayers composed by the Queen in several languages, and her speech to the audience almost at the end of the last scene of all is derived from her so-called Golden Speech to Parliament. The allusions to her intelligence service as her 'eyes and ears', and to her dress figured with representations of those organs, were suggested by the famous portrait at Hatfield, which Lord Salisbury was good enough to show, among other treasures, to the composer and the librettist.

*   *   *

Lute Song

> Happy were he could finish forth his fate
> In some unhaunted desert, where, obscure
> From all society, from love and hate
> Of worldly folk, then might he sleep secure;
> Then wake again, and give God ever praise,
> Content with hips and haws and brambleberry;
> In contemplation spending all his days,
> And chance of holy thoughts to make him merry:
> Where, when he dies, his tomb might be a bush
> Where harmless Robin dwells with gentle thrush . . .

> Robert Devereux, Earl of Essex

Shirley Chapman as Lady Essex, Ava June as Elizabeth, Norman Welsby as Cecil in the ENO production on the visit to the 1975 Vienna Festival (photos: Donald Southern)

Gloriana

An Opera in Three Acts
by William Plomer
Music by Benjamin Britten

This work is dedicated by gracious permission to
Her Majesty Queen Elizabeth II
in honour of whose Coronation
it was composed.

Gloriana was first performed at Covent Garden on June 8, 1953. The
first performance in the USA was a concert performance in Cincinatti
on May 8, 1956.

Joan Cross as Elizabeth in the Covent Garden première (photo: Roger Wood)

CHARACTERS

Queen Elizabeth the First	*soprano*
Robert Devereux *Earl of Essex*	*tenor*
Frances *Countess of Essex*	*mezzo-soprano*
Charles Blount *Lord Mountjoy*	*baritone*
Penelope (Lady Rich) *sister to Essex*	*soprano*
Sir Robert Cecil* *Secretary of the Council*	*baritone*
Sir Walter Raleigh* *Captain of the Guard*	*baritone*
Henry Cuffe *a satellite of Essex*	*baritone*
A Lady-in-waiting	*soprano*
A blind ballad-singer	*bass*
The Recorder of Norwich	*bass*
A housewife	*mezzo-soprano*
The Spirit of the Masque	*tenor*
The Master of Ceremonies	*tenor*
The City Crier	*baritone*

Chorus: Citizens, Maids of Honour, Ladies and Gentlemen of the Household, Courtiers, Masquers, Old Men, Men and Boys of Essex's Following, Councillors.

Dancers: Time, Concord, Country Girls, Rustics, Fishermen, Morris Dancer.

Actors: Pages, Ballad-Singer's Runner, Phantom of Queen Elizabeth.

Musicians on Stage: State Trumpeters, Dance Orchestra, Pipe and Tabor, Gittern, Drummer.

England in the time of Queen Elizabeth I. The later years of her reign, which lasted from 1558 to 1603.

* *Pronunciation Note:* Throughout the opera Cecil should be *Cicil* and Raleigh should be *Rawleigh*.

104

Act One

Scene One. / *No. 1 Prelude* / *Outside a tilting-ground during a tournament. Essex, attended by Cuffe, is listening to the proceedings within. Cuffe, at an opening, reports on what he can see.* / *No. 2 The tournament.*

CHORUS
(*off*)

What champion rides?
Is it Mountjoy?

CUFFE

He throws the gauntlet down!

ESSEX

Who throws the gauntlet down?

CUFFE

He takes it up!

ESSEX

Who takes it up?

CUFFE

My lord Mountjoy.

ESSEX

Oh, if his luck were mine!

CHORUS

He mounts in hope,
With joy we cheer! Mountjoy!

CUFFE

They both salute the Queen.

CHORUS

Hail!

ESSEX

Why do they cheer?

CUFFE

My lord, they love the sight of him.

ESSEX

I hear they do.
If only I were he!

CHORUS

Our joy mounts up,
Our hope, Mountjoy!

CUFFE

They're in the lists, about to charge!
They charge!
A glancing blow –
Will you not watch, my lord?

ESSEX

If I should watch
I could not bear to see
Mountjoy prevail.

CHORUS

Strike anew,
Strike once more!
Mountjoy! Our joy!

CUFFE

They wheel and turn,
He parries with his shield!
A giant thrust! He reels!

ESSEX

Say that he falls,
Say that Mountjoy falls!

CHORUS

Our hope falls!
Mountjoy, our hope sustain!

CUFFE

He does not fall!
Again he wheels for the charge,
Once more they ride.

ESSEX

This time he falls!
This time he's down!

CHORUS

Strike now, Mountjoy!
Mountjoy!

CUFFE

My lord he's down!

ESSEX

Who's down?

CUFFE

With one great blow
Against his iron breast
The other is unhorsed!

ESSEX

I cannot bear his luck!

CUFFE

Mountjoy has won!

CHORUS

Our champion now
We cheer Mountjoy!
Mountjoy!

CUFFE

There now
The mob has all gone wild
Because Mountjoy has won!

ESSEX

Mountjoy has won!

CHORUS

Mountjoy! Mountjoy!

CUFFE

Now he makes his humble duty
Before the Queen in strength and beauty.

ESSEX

His the place that should be mine!

CHORUS

Dismounts with joy,
Salutes the Queen!

CUFFE

He takes a golden prize
Now from the royal hand.

ESSEX

Ah!

CHORUS

Mountjoy!

CUFFE

To the Queen like one they are turning.

CHORUS [7a]

Green leaves are we,
Red rose our golden Queen,
O crownèd rose among the leaves so green.

Mountjoy emerges from a tent, accompanied by a Page, to whom he hands the golden chessman just presented to him by the Queen, together with a crimson ribbon.

MOUNTJOY

Boy, bind upon my arm
This my reward.

PAGE

My lord!

He does so, with the ribbon.

MOUNTJOY

I'll wear it as a charm:
No sooner said than done.

No. 3 Recitative and Fight

ESSEX

'Twas you, my lord Mountjoy,
That won the crowd?
It was. I know it. And I know
Easy applause is loud.

MOUNTJOY

My friend, I boast not.

ESSEX

No,
You need not!

MOUNTJOY

Need not?

ESSEX

What meaneth, may I ask,
That bauble on your arm?

MOUNTJOY

It is a golden queen at chess
The Queen herself as prize
Gave me in great goodwill.
Take back those words!
Unsay it, then!

ESSEX

You find in that your happiness?
Mere luck I must despise!
A favour now for every fool!
Not I!
A favour for a fool, I said!
Not I!
Nay!

They draw their swords and fight. [5] A fanfare is sounded off. Essex turns at the sound, and receives a slight wound in the left arm. Enter Trumpeteers. [6] Essex's Page binds a scarf round his arm; the scarf at once appears blood-stained. To the sound of the trumpets a procession emerges from the tilting ground, and is followed by a crowd. Essex and Mountjoy kneel as the Queen appears, attended by Raleigh. / No. 4 Entrance of the Queen

QUEEN
(*in surprise and concern*)

Heaven what have we here?
A wound! My Lord of Essex bleedeth!
(*Seeing at once that the wound is not grave, she turns to Raleigh and speaks ironically.*)
One lord weareth a favour,
The other weareth a wound!
How now?

CHORUS

One lord another supersedeth, –
Rivals for a lady's favour!

The Queen turns to Essex.

QUEEN

You did not get
That mark in sport!

Essex bows and makes no reply. / No. 5 Recitative

QUEEN

The Earl of Essex hangs his head,
Hath lost his tongue, forgot
His courtliness as well. Beware!
I'll not be crossed!

106

We'll have you both to know
An ancient rule: at court
No man may strike a blow
For any cause at all.

She turns to Mountjoy.

Hearken, my lord Mountjoy:
What penalty should fall
On noble lords who strive
Like ostlers in a brawl?

Explain yourselves!
I'll have the gist!
Your Prince commands!

CHORUS

Her Majesty will hear their case.

QUEEN

I command you!

No. 6 The two lords' explanation

MOUNTJOY
(to the Queen)

The honour done me by your Grace
Hath been dishonoured in this place!
(to Essex)
I flaunted nothing,
You intruded!
Meek am I,
To hear accusings?

ESSEX
(to the Queen)

The honour done him by your Grace
He came and flaunted in my face!
(to Mountjoy)
A dolt am I
To be deluded?
Or craven I,
To bear abusings?

ESSEX AND MOUNTJOY

The royal presence must subdue
My rightful rage!

QUEEN

Halt! In Heaven's name be dumb!
Even when fishwives wrangle
They must make an end of words.

CHORUS

The Queen will have them know their place!

The Queen turns to Raleigh.

QUEEN

Raleigh! What think you
Of these pettish lords?

CHORUS

Sir Walter takes them both to task.

RALEIGH

As your Highness commands,
Let me, of riper age,
Tell what I see.

No. 7 Raleigh's Song

Both lords are younglings, both
In glory would appear:
'Stay,' quoth the first one,
'What dost thou here?'
'Pride,' doth the other answer,
'Brings you, my lord, too near'.

These two are rivals, like
The blue fly and the bee:
'Buzz,' quoth the blue fly,
'Hum,' quoth the bee,
'How can this busybody
Take precedence of me?'

When head and heart are hot
Then tongue and hand are wild:
So, Ma'am, it looks to me.

ESSEX AND MOUNTJOY
(aside)

I curse him for his insolence,
And some day I will hurl him down.

No. 8 Ensemble of Reconciliation

QUEEN

Raleigh, your wit flies free,
We find your judgment mild.
(She turns to Mountjoy and Essex.)
Approach, my subjects both,
And hear my judgment now.

CHORUS

Like Solomon, the wisest Prince,
Our Prince her wisdom to her judgment
  brings.

Essex and Mountjoy approach the Queen.

QUEEN

Anger would be too strong
Against this youthful sparring:
My ruling hear ye both:
Forbear from graver warring!

God's death, we need your arms!
Pray you, good lords, defend us,
Our kingdom and our people
Against the foes would end us.

Fail not to come to court   [3]
In fine or dirty weather,
I'll not neglect you –
But see you come together!

Rise both, my lords, and see
How these good folk respect you:
Spurn not their trust; remember
Your Princess will protect you.

ESSEX AND MOUNTJOY

She'll not neglect us
If we will come together.

RALEIGH AND CUFFE

Fail not to come to court
In fine or dirty weather.

CHORUS

Fail not to come to court
In fine or dirty weather:
She'll not neglect them
If they will come together.

To our great Queen,
Our Queen,
Thanks we now give.

ESSEX

The wisdom of our Queen
Hath made us brothers,
Who this day were foes.

MOUNTJOY

Our quarrel over, I engage
Myself to be his friend.

CUFFE

In thankfulness your servant,
I stand in a lower place.

RALEIGH

All honour to our Queen, who calms
The stubborn knights-at-arms.

ESSEX

If Gloriana gives me armies to command,
My banner will emblazon lasting love.

MOUNTJOY

A loyal homage is a lasting love
In one that offers life to her.

CUFFE

Obeying such a monarch
Raiseth a man's esteem.

RALEIGH

Each heart from now be dedicate
Unto this wise Princess.

CHORUS

The wisdom of our Queen
Hath made them brothers
Who this day were foes

ESSEX, MOUNTJOY, RALEIGH AND CUFFE

Our lives are in your hand,
Queen of this island region!
Your life is guarded
By ours as by a legion:
We vow this day.

ALL
(*except the Queen*)

Long may she keep this realm
From war and war's alarms!
Green leaves are we,   [7a]
Red rose our golden Queen,
O crownèd rose among the leaves so green!

*Essex and Mountjoy kneel at the Queen's
feet. She removes her glove, and gives her
hand to Essex, and then to Mountjoy, who
both kiss it.)*

QUEEN

And now I give you both
My hand, for your obedience.

ESSEX AND MOUNTJOY

Your Majesty, a subject kneels
To thank you for your grace.

No. 9 Recitative and Final March

QUEEN

My lords, your quarrel's reconciled,
And now I end this audience.
Let trumpets blow!

ESSEX, MOUNTJOY AND RALEIGH

Let trumpets blow!

QUEEN, ESSEX, MOUNTJOY AND RALEIGH

Lead on!

*The trumpets start a march and the company
company moves off in procession.*

Curtain.

Scene Two. *A private apartment at
Nonesuch. The Queen is alone with Cecil.
She is seated. He is standing. / No. 1
Prelude and Dialogue*

QUEEN

Too touchy and too hot,
They fought like boys.
Lady Rich, Penelope,
What did she say or do
When she heard of the fight?

CECIL

My lord of Essex is her brother;
My lady was much concerned.

QUEEN

Concerned for both?

CECIL

Madam, rumour declares
Mountjoy and Lady Rich are closely fond.

QUEEN

'Tis true, I know: the dark Penelope!
To have a brother and a lover fight
Would banish all tranquillity.

CECIL

The touchier of the two received the wound.

QUEEN

'Twas right someone should take
Our Essex down,
Or he might grow unruly, and unruled.

CECIL

The Earl will not be schooled,
Will never learn restraint.

QUEEN

My pigmy elf, ah! 'tis for that
I love the lordly boy!

CECIL

Ah, Madam, pray take care!

No. 2 The Queen's Song

QUEEN

Hark, sir! This ring
I had at my crowning:
With it I wedded
Myself to the realm.

My comfort hath been
That my people are happy:
Happiness theirs
Because you are discreet.

I seek no husband:
But good Master Ascham
In my infancy taught me
Love's better than fear.

CECIL

And caution is better,
Sweet Highness, than ruin,
Than rashness and ruin!
O Princess, whom your people love
As their protector, long and long
My noble father served you:
O let me serve you now, recite
The precept that my father taught!

No. 3 Cecil's Song of Government [4]

The art of government
Is in procrastination and
   In silence and delay:
Blazing bonfires left to burn
Will soon consume themselves away.

Of evils choose the least:
Great foes will tumble down in time,
   Or wither, one by one:
He that rules must hear and see
What's openly or darkly done.

And *that* is not enough:
There comes a moment when to rule
   Is to be swift and bold:
Know at last the time to strike –
It may be when the iron is cold!

QUEEN

Your Princess thanks you, trusty elf.

No. 4 Recitative and Essex's Entry

CECIL

Now if I may obtrude myself,
The new Ambassador from Spain –

QUEEN

Is at the old one's tricks again!   [10]
With one care ended, others are begun.

CECIL

The newest is an old care now renewed.

QUEEN

What new old care is this?

CECIL

Word has been brought
The King of Spain designs
A new Armada to be sent –

QUEEN

How soon?
How nearly can they guess,
Our faithful eyes and ears?

CECIL

Perhaps before the spring.

QUEEN

God's death! What men,
What money must be thrown
Into the maw of cannon!

CECIL

Madam, we are in the hands of God.
He at a breath can melt the steel of Spain:
We can but watch and wait.

QUEEN

We can but watch and wait.

A page enters.

PAGE

My lord of Essex!

*Essex entres, kneels and rises. The page goes
out.*

QUEEN

Welcome, my lord. Sir Robert here,
So wise in counsel, will return anon.
      (*Cecil bows himself out.*)
Cousin, I greet you.

ESSEX

Queen of my life!

QUEEN

Ah, Robin!

ESSEX

Queen of my life!   [11]

QUEEN

Cares of State eat up my days.
There lies my lute;
Take it and play.

No. 5 First Lute Song [12]

ESSEX
(*taking up the lute*)

   Quick music is best
When the heart is oppressed;
   Quick music can heal
With dancing, by night and by day.
Hallalloo, hallallay.

   Quick music is best
For the pipe or the strings;

109

Quick music can heal
With dancing, the pleasure of kings.
Hallalloo, hallallay.

QUEEN

Too light, too gay:
A song for careless hearts.
Turn to the lute again,
Evoke some far-off place or time,
A dream, a mood, an air
To spirit us both away.

No. 6 Second Lute Song [13]

ESSEX

Happy were he could finish forth his fate
In some unhaunted desert, where, obscure
From all society, from love and hate
Of worldly folk, then might he sleep secure;
Then wake again, and give God ever praise,
Content with hips and haws and bramble-
     berry;
In contemplation spending all his days,
And change of holy thoughts to make him
     merry;
Where, when he dies, his tomb might be a
     bush
Where harmless Robin dwells with gentle
     thrush;
                                   Happy were he!

QUEEN

Robin, a melting song: but who
Can this unworldly hermit be?

ESSEX

It might be any man, not one you know.

QUEEN

'Tis a conceit, it is not you.

*No. 7 The First Duet for the Queen and
Essex*

ESSEX
(*putting the lute aside*)

Queen of my life, I cannot tell.

QUEEN

You man of moods!

ESSEX

I know it well!

QUEEN

Victor of Cadiz!

ESSEX

Loser of esteem!

QUEEN

Leader of armies!

ESSEX

Follower of a dream!

QUEEN

Now up, now down, and cautious never!

ESSEX

But to one passion constant ever!

QUEEN

To advance in fortune, as becomes a man.

ESSEX

To advance in favour, as a suitor longs.

QUEEN

Do I not favour thee,
Promote thy pride
And right thy wrongs?

ESSEX

Sovereign most loved –

What solace more
Can I disclose?
Better than tears the faithfulness I bring,
What my heart holds, only thy heart knows:
And I too now can sing:
Are tears a sign to show
That we shall reap but as we sow?

QUEEN

O heretofore
Though ringed with foes,
I only bed with arrows of the spring,
My sense was only wounded by the rose:
And I too then could sing:
But years decline and go:
Video et taceo!

ESSEX

Ah, Madam, than your voice with me
No song is sweeter.

QUEEN

Then rejoice with me!
I am a woman, though I be a Queen,
And still a woman, though I be a Prince!

ESSEX

Then let me dare assert
     The man I am, avow
Mine humble duty is
     Far more than duty now:

Call me not malapert
     If from thy feet I start
A subject, who declares
     A more than subject heart –

QUEEN

Robin, no more!
Blow not the spark to flame –
Look, my lord, we are not alone!

*She points to the silhouette of Raleigh
suddenly visible through the curtain.*

ESSEX

The jackal lurking by the wall,   [14]
How vain his hope the lion will fall!

QUEEN

Be less impetuous, my lord.

ESSEX

The jackal waiting in the night,
He keepeth long his evil spite.

QUEEN

You wrong Sir Walter Raleigh there.

ESSEX

Raleigh, Cecil, seek to ban
My claim to Ireland, if they can.
I am the man to conquer
Tyrone. For God's sake let me go!
I am the man Tyrone to overthrow,
Sweet Prince, for God's sake let me go!

QUEEN

Your 'plainings I can ne'er refuse.
    (*She strikes a bell.*)
Robin, I must spare your presence:
The business of the kingdom waits.
Make your adieux!

*Raleigh's shadow vanishes. Essex kneels,
and she gives him her hand to kiss. The page
appears, and Essex bows himself out. / No.
8 Soliloquy and Prayer*

QUEEN
(*soliloquizing*)

On rivalries 'tis safe for kings   [7b]
To base their power: but how their spirit
    longs
For harmonies and mellowings

Of discords harsh, of real and phantom
    wrongs!
        (*thinking of Essex*)
If life were love and love were true,
Then could I love thee through and through!
        (*with sudden resolution*)
But God gave me a sceptre,
    The burden and the glory –
I must not lay them down:
    I live and reign a virgin,
        Will die in honour,
Leave a refulgent crown!

(*In a rapt, exalted mood, she kneels and
prays aloud.*)

O God, my King, sole ruler of the world,
That pulled me from a prison to a palace
To be a sovereign Princess
And to rule the people of England:

Thou hast placed me high, but my flesh is
    frail:
Without Thee my throne is unstable,
My kingdom tottering, my life uncertain:
Oh maintain in this weak woman the heart
    of a man!

Errors and faults have beset me from my
    youth,
I bow myself before the throne of Thy
    grace;
Forgive and protect me, O God, my King,
That I may rule and protect my people in
    peace.

                        Amen.

Slow Curtain.

*Gwynne Howell as Raleigh in the
1972 Sadler's Wells production
(photo: Donald Southern)*

Act Two

Scene One. *The Guildhall at Norwich.*
The Queen is on progress through the city.
She is attended by Raleigh, Cecil, Essex,
Mountjoy and gentlemen of the Court. She
is listening to the conclusion of an address by
the Recorder in the presence of a crowd. /
No. 1 Prelude and Welcome

RECORDER

And therefore, most gracious Empress, the
citizens of Norwich must always pray for
Your Majesty's royal person, whom God,
now and ever, preserve, to His good
pleasure and our great comfort.

QUEEN

I thank you, Master Recorder. You have
spoken to me from the faithful hearts of my
people of Norwich, and I would have them
know that they may have a greater or wiser
prince, but they shall never have a prince
more loving.

CROWD

Hurrah! Hurrah!

The Recorder approaches the Queen, who
gives him her hand to kiss. In attempting to
kneel before her, he stumbles. She helps him
to rise.

QUEEN

Good sir, your homage hath nearly proved
your undoing.

RECORDER

Madam, forgive me.
My bones are old;
My heart is old,
But not too old to beat,
And if my knees would bend
I would be kneeling at your feet.

QUEEN

God's blessing on your heart, continue
　　there.

CROWD

Behold! Behold!
Never was a prince more loving!

RECORDER

Madam, it is our hope
You may be pleased to see
A masque, here new devised
To honour you, with song and dance.

The Queen signifies her consent, and is
conducted to a chair. She is facing a fanciful
leafy bower specially made for the occasion.

ESSEX
(aside)

Tedious orations, dotards on their knees –
I for one could yawn myself to death.

CECIL
(aside)

To be on progress with her Majesty,
Is that no honour to you now, my lord?

ESSEX

An honour, yes, but like a chain
That holds me back.

CECIL

That holds you back, from what?

ESSEX

When will the Queen decide
Her Deputy for Ireland?

CECIL

The masque begins.

No. 2 The Masque

MASQUERS
(semi-chorus)

Melt earth to sea, sea flow to air,
And air fly into fire!
The elements, at Gloriana's chair,
Mingle in tuneful choir.

SPIRIT OF THE MASQUE

And now we summon from this leafy bower
The demi-god that must appear!
'Tis Time! 'Tis Time!

From the bower springs forth a sunburnt
and heroic-looking young man representing
Time. He carries a bag slung from one
shoulder. Time dances. / First Dance

MASQUERS

Yes, he is Time,
Lusty and blithe!
　　Time is at his apogee,
Although you thought to see
A bearded ancient with a scythe.

No reaper he
That cries 'Take heed!'
　　Time is at his apogee!
Young and strong, in his prime:
Behold the sower of the seed!

QUEEN
(aside)

And Time it was that brought me here.

ESSEX
(aside)

And Time hath yet to bring me what is due.

SPIRIT OF THE MASQUE

Time could not sow unless
He had a spouse to bless
His work, and give it life –
Concord, his loving wife!

*From the bower steps forth Concord, a
young woman of placid beauty. She dances.
/ Second Dance*

MASQUERS

Concord is here
Our days to bless
And this our land to endue
With plenty, peace and happiness.

Concord and Time
Each needeth each:
The ripest fruit hangs where
Not one, but only two can reach.

SPIRIT OF THE MASQUE

Now Time with Concord dances
This island doth rejoice:
And woods and waves and waters
Make echo to our voice.

*Time and Concord dance together. / Third
Dance*

MASQUERS

From springs of bounty
Through this county
Streams abundant
Of thanks shall flow!
Where life was scanty
Fruits of plenty
Swell resplendent
From earth below!

No Greek nor Roman,
Queenly woman
Knew such favour
From Heaven above
As she whose presence
Is our pleasance:
Gloriana
Hath all our love!

RALEIGH
(aside)

My lord, hath time brought concord now
  between
The Earl of Essex and yourself?

MOUNTJOY
(aside)

Again we are good friends.

RALEIGH

He loves me not.
Take with a grain of salt,
I beg you, his abuse of me.

SPIRIT OF THE MASQUE

And now, country maidens, bring a tribute
of flowers to the flower of princes all.

*A troop of Young Girls step lightly out from
the bower, and dance. / Fourth Dance*

MASQUERS

Sweet flag and cuckoo-flower,
Cowslip and columbine,
King-cups and sops-in-wine,
Flower-de-luce and calaminth,
Harebell and hyacinth,
Myrtle and bay, with rosemary between,
Norfolk's own garlands for her Queen!

SPIRIT OF THE MASQUE

Behold a troop of rustic swains, bringing
from the waves and pastures the fruits of
their toil.

*A troop of Rustics and Fishermen appear
from the bower. They dance. / Fifth Dance*

MASQUERS

From fen and meadow
In rushy baskets
They bring ensamples
Of all they grow:
In earthen dishes
Their deep-sea-fishes;
Yearling fleeces,
Woven blankets;
New cream and junkets,
And rustic trinkets
On wicker flaskets,
Their country largess—
The best they know!

SPIRIT OF THE MASQUE

Led by Time and Concord, let all unite in
homage to Gloriana, our hope of peace, our
flower of grace.

*A sixth and final dance, in which all the
performers join.*

SPIRIT OF THE MASQUE AND MASQUERS

These tokens of our love receiving,
Oh take them, Princess great and dear,
From Norwich, city you are leaving,
That you afar may feel us near.

QUEEN

Norwich, we never can forget,
Where Time and Concord sweetly met:
Good folk, we thank you from our heart,
And in your time may concord ne'er depart.

CHORUS AND MASQUERS

Behold! Never was a Prince more loving.
O crownèd rose among the leaves so green!
Hurrah! Hurrah!

THE QUEEN'S ATTENDANTS

Long live our rose, our evergreen!

Slow Curtain.

Scene Two. *The garden of Essex House in the Strand. Evening. Mountjoy is alone.* /
No. 1 *Prelude and Song*

MOUNTJOY

A garden by a river at a trysting
Is perfect in the evening for a pair,
Yet if one for the other long attendeth,
Delay falls like a frost upon the air.

But anguish is exquisite in waiting,
And who, with hope aflame, who feeleth
   chill?
And oh, who can say, when waiting endeth,
There is more joy in hunting than the kill?

Lady Rich appears.

My dark Penelope!

LADY RICH

Mountjoy, I am here at last
For a stolen hour by the Thames:
And stolen love demandeth
Crafty stratagems!

MOUNTJOY

An angel wedded to a brute!

LADY RICH

But could an angel so deceive?

No. 2 *Duet*

MOUNTJOY AND LADY RICH

Let us walk in the paths of pleasure
And forget the nagging world outside:

MOUNTJOY

My rare one, my ruby, my treasure,
My stealthy, my secret one, my bride!

LADY RICH

Thy words are honey-dew to me:
I never hear their like from my lord.

MOUNTJOY

I'll give thee more than words.

LADY RICH

And more than words I will return thee.

MOUNTJOY

Come to the fountain, my Penelope.

LADY RICH

Yes, I will come with thee.

MOUNTJOY AND LADY RICH

And watch our two reflections kiss:
There in the water we shall see
The double image of our single bliss.
Waters, like mirrors, have no memory
Of any strange encounters they reflect.

*Essex and Lady Essex appear. They do not
see Mountjoy and Lady Rich, but are
watched by them.* / No. 3 *Double Duet*

ESSEX

Whatever step I take
The Queen will bar my way.

LADY ESSEX

The Queen knows your valour!

ESSEX

She knoweth not
How quick my patience ebbs.

LADY ESSEX

A subject must obey.

ESSEX

Caprice, rebuff, delay—

Essex and Lady Essex move out of sight.

MOUNTJOY

Your brother weareth sorrow like a mask.

LADY RICH

He feels his strength unused:
With a great army he would sail
To Ireland, to attack Tyrone:
And he will mope or storm until
The Queen hath let him go.

MOUNTJOY AND LADY RICH

A garden by the river in the evening
Is doleful for a man ill at ease,
With enemies whose envy is more sombre
Than cold unfathomed hollows of the seas.

Essex and Lady Essex re-appear.

ESSEX

Caprice, rebuff, delay—
Far more than enough to bear.

LADY ESSEX

In time she must relent.

ESSEX

In time! I'll break her will! I'll have my way!

LADY ESSEX

Robert, beware! You might be heard!

*Mountjoy and Lady Rich come out of the
shadows.*

MOUNTJOY AND LADY RICH

Essex, } you might be heard
Brother } By other ears than ours.

LADY ESSEX

Penelope! My lord Mountjoy!

ESSEX

On my own ground,
With my own voice,
To my own wife
I dare indict
Council and Queen,
And Heaven itself —

114

LADY ESSEX

No, my good lord,
You do blaspheme!

ESSEX

'Tis them I hate,
And Cecil first,
The hunchback fox;
Raleigh I curse;
The Queen I blame.

LADY RICH AND MOUNTJOY

My lord, we know you have
Reasons and rights.

ESSEX

By Heav'n, my voice deserveth to be heard!
My birth and rank alone should make me
first preferred:
How long am I to wait? The Queen shall
know
Delay may turn a sweet affection sour.

LADY RICH

Call on the stars above
To give us one great hour
And the force to shape our fate!
I with the power of love,
You with the love of power,
We can seize the reins of State!

LADY ESSEX

Oh be cautious, I implore you!
These are treasonable words.
Danger is all about us,
Danger to all we love.

LADY RICH, ESSEX AND MOUNTJOY

The Queen is old, and time will steal
Sceptre and orb from out her hand.
Ours to decide
What other head shall wear the crown;
Ours to maintain
Our hold upon the helm of State.

LADY ESSEX

Oh pray be cautious, I implore you!
We have great enemies.

LADY RICH, ESSEX AND MOUNTJOY

Yet not so great as our resolve
Ourselves to rule the land.

Curtain.

Scene Three. *A great room in the Palace
of Whitehall at night. An orchestra is playing
in the gallery. Courtiers and their Ladies are
assembled, and a pavane is being danced. /
No. 1 Pavane / When it ends, the dancers
and onlookers converse. / No. 2 Conversation*

CHORUS

Pavanes so grave and dignified . . .
Slow and solemn . . .

Too slow for the young . . .
The very harbinger of State . . .

*Essex and Lady Essex enter, followed by
Lady Rich and Mountjoy. Lady Essex is
more splendidly dressed than any other lady
present, and at once attracts attention.*

LADY-IN-WAITING

In homage to the Queen, no doubt,
My Lady Essex is so fine tonight.

LADY RICH

In homage to the Queen,
To her Lord, my brother,
To honour all of us:
And how my lady shines!

MOUNTJOY

Frances, bright star of night,
All eyes to you are turning.

LADY ESSEX

Robert would have me blaze,
In all this gaudiness:
But will the Queen approve?

ESSEX

Earl Marshal of England, I require
My lady to appear in state
Befitting her rank and beauty.

*A tabor in the gallery sounds at a signal
from the Master of Ceremonies.*

MASTER OF CEREMONIES

May it please you to dance a galliard!

*A galliard is danced, in which Essex and
Lady Essex take part, and in which Lady
Rich is partnered by Mountjoy. / No. 3
Galiard / As it ends, the dancers and
onlookers converse. / No. 4 Conversation
and the Queen's Entrance*

CHORUS

Courtly dancing the heart rejoices . . .
Graceful gliding . . .
Brave looks, noble, noble measure . . .
Nothing is lacking but the Queen . . .

*The Queen enters, and is received with
deep bows and curtsies. She catches sight of
Lady Essex and looks her up and down for a
perceptible moment.*

QUEEN

On hot nights and for stately moods
Pavanes and galliards are all very well.
Tonight the air is chilly,
So let us warm our blood
By dancing high
In the Italian mode.
Command there a lavolta!

The tabor sounds as before.

MASTER OF CEREMONIES

May it please you to dance lavolta!

A lavolta is danced, the Queen showing great energy and spirit. / No. 5 Lavolta / As it ends, the dancers and onlookers exclaim with animation, while fluttering fans and mopping their faces with handkerchiefs. / No. 6 Conversation

CHORUS

Lusty leaping! Jump for joy! . . .
Leg over leg, as the dog went to Dover . . .
Gay go up, and gay go down . . .
And the cow jumped over the moon! . . .

QUEEN

High stepping rejoices the sinews
And for a long life the wise decree
A free and frequent sweat.
The ladies will change their linen!
And presently I will rejoin you.

The Queen goes out, followed by the ladies who have been dancing, among them Lady Essex. A tiny Morris Dancer, his face blacked, comes in to entertain the company during the interval before the ladies return. / No. 7 Morris Dance / The last of the ladies to return is Lady Essex, now wearing a plain dress. / No. 8 Recitative

LADY RICH

Frances, so plain now?
So late and breathless?

LADY ESSEX

While I was changing
My new court dress vanished;
The maid came running, saying
It was nowhere to be found.

LADY RICH

Some prank has been played on you. Ah!

The Queen suddenly returns, unheralded and unattended, and wearing Lady Essex's missing dress. It is much too short for her, and she looks grotesque. / No. 9 The Queen's Burlesque

QUEEN

Well, ladies, how like you
My new-fancied suit?

The ladies look at one another in uncertainty and amazement, and curtsey to the Queen. The courtiers bow, murmur among themselves, and shrink back.

QUEEN
(*turning round once or twice like a mannequin*)

My new-fancied suit!

The Queen moves slowly, posturing and turning herself this way and that, towards Lady Essex on the far side of the stage.

Ah, now, my lady,
And what think you?

Too short, is it not?
And becometh me ill?

LADY ESSEX
(*distressed and embarrassed*)

May it please your Majesty –

QUEEN

It pleaseth me not!
If, being too short,
It becometh not me,
I have it in mind
It can ne'er become thee
As being too gaudy!
So choose we another!

She slowly stalks out, amid bowings and curtseyings. Lady Essex turns away and hides her face in her hands. She is a little apart from the rest of the company. / No. 10 Quartet [2]

ESSEX, MOUNTJOY AND LADY RICH
(*approaching Lady Essex*)

Good Frances, do not weep.

ESSEX

The Queen upon herself hath brought
Shame, and not upon my lady here.

LADY RICH

Envy and pride inflame the Queen.

ESSEX AND LADY RICH

Good Frances, do not weep.

MOUNTJOY

My lady, in whatever garb
Your sweet grace is clad,
No man on earth dare cast
A slight, or slighting look
Upon an inch of it.

ESSEX

True, my friend,
But no man has done so.

LADY RICH

Oh see what comes of being ruled –

ESSEX AND MOUNTJOY

By a king in a farthingale!

ESSEX, LADY RICH AND MOUNTJOY

Good Frances, do not weep.

LADY ESSEX

My friends, take care:
Her sudden rage is over now.

ESSEX

Who last year struck me with her hand
Before her Council!
Who taunts my wife before her Court!

LADY ESSEX

She is the Queen!

ESSEX

No spiteful woman ever born
Shall with impunity do this!

LADY ESSEX

Robert, take care:
She is the Queen,
And as the Queen
Hath her conditions.

ESSEX

Conditions! Conditions!
Her conditions are as crooked as her carcass!

ESSEX, LADY RICH AND MOUNTJOY

Ah!

MASTER OF CEREMONIES

My lords and ladies, make way
For the Queen and her Councillors!

*No. 11 A march. / The Queen returns in
state, arrayed now in her own clothes. She is
attended by Cecil, Raleigh, and councillors. /
No. 12 The Queen's Announcement*

RALEIGH

My Lord of Essex, I am commanded by the
Queen to summon you hither to her
presence that you may hear a matter of
great moment.

*Essex, surprised, uneasy, still enraged, and
feeling guilty after his outburst, approaches
the Queen with a defiant and truculent air,
then abruptly kneels. Cecil hands the Queen
a paper:*

QUEEN

My lord of Essex, Knight of our most noble
Order of the Garter, Earl Marshal of
England, our trusty and well-beloved
Cousin. Here in the presence of our
Council, of the Captain of our Guard, and
our Court assembled, here acquaint you
that by our Letters Patent you are this day
appointed Lord Deputy in Ireland. You are
to conquer the rebel Tyrone, who en-
courageth our enemies in Spain and
grievously wasteth our substance.
(She hands the paper back to Cecil.)
Go! Go into Ireland, and bring back victory
and peace!

*She extends her hand, which Essex kisses
fervently. / No. 13 Ensemble*

CHORUS

Victor of Cadiz,
    Overcome Tyrone!
All Spain will cower
    When the rebel falls!

RALEIGH
(*aside*)

So now he has his way,
So goes he to his fate.

CECIL
(*aside*)

Exalted high among his peers,
He may at last more steeply fall.

QUEEN

There, Robin, go!

CHORUS

Victor of Cadiz,
    Overcome Tyrone!
All Spain will cower
    When the rebel falls!

MOUNTJOY AND LADY RICH
(*aside*)

Returning soon, oh soon,
With armies at his back,
He then will hold
The kingdom in his hand.

LADY ESSEX

At last the Queen
Drives all his cares away.
The load that I have borne
Is not so grievous now.

CHORUS

Go, warlike Earl, for Gloriana, go!

QUEEN

England and England's Queen
Entrust their hopes to you.

CHORUS

Victor of Cadiz,
    Overcome Tyrone!
Come back in triumph
    To these shouting halls!

ESSEX

Armed with the favour of our gracious
Empress, I am armed like a god. My
resolve and duty are my helm and sword,
the hopes of my countrymen are my spurs.
And so into Ireland I go, to break for ever
those rebel kerns. With God's help I will
have victory, and you shall have peace.

QUEEN

Tomorrow to your charge:
Tonight we dance.
Strike up the music!

MASTER OF CEREMONIES

May it please you to dance a coranto!

QUEEN

Robert, your hand!

*Essex leads the Queen in a coranto, and
other couples follow. / No. 14 Coranto*

Slow Curtain.

Act Three

Scene One. *An anteroom to the Queen's dressing-room at Nonesuch. At the back a curtain. Early morning. Maids of Honour in conversation. / No. 1 Prelude and Chatter* [15]

FIRST GROUP

What news from Ireland?

SECOND GROUP

Delay, delay; a sorry farce!
The summer wasted, then a truce.

FIRST GROUP

We thought by now to see the rebel's head
Laid at the Queen's feet.

ALL

Her darling Robin hath betrayed her hopes.

SECOND GROUP

The Queen knows more than we.

FIRST GROUP

Knows everything: they say
She used to have a dress
Figured from neck to hem with eyes and ears.

ALL

Ah, she is wary and wise
In the ways of the world!

SECOND GROUP

Those tiring-maids are mighty slow.

FIRST GROUP

As a woman ages
She needeth more artifice
To deck her fading bloom!

ALL

You'll come to it yourself!

Enter Lady-in-Waiting in some agitation.

ALL

What now?

LADY-IN-WAITING

What now? Is the Queen dressed?
There's a great stir below!
Horsemen in haste and urgent words,
Running footsteps and panic fear!
I fear bad news
Or some complot against the Queen –

No. 2 Essex's Intrusion

ALL

O God, what's this?

Essex bursts in, wild-looking, travel-stained, with his hand on his sword. The Maids of Honour are alarmed and recoil. The Lady-in-Waiting steps forward to meet him and try and restrain him.

LADY-IN-WAITING

My lord!

ESSEX

Is the Queen up?
Is the Queen yet dressed?

LADY-IN-WAITING

My lord!

ESSEX

I must see the Queen!

LADY-IN-WAITING

My lord, forbear awhile:
The Queen is not yet dressed.

ESSEX

I cannot wait!

LADY-IN-WAITING

The Queen, my lord, cannot receive you now!

ESSEX

She must!
(*The Maids of Honour try to bar his way.*)
Ladies, prevent me not!

He steps forward and sweeps the curtain back, disclosing the Queen seated at her dressing-table, wearing an old, plain dressing-gown. Two Tiring-Maids are standing beside her, helping her to dress. Her red-gold wig is on a stand before her, among the paraphernalia of the toilet. She has a looking-glass in her hand. Directly she sees Essex she puts the looking-glass down. / No. 3 The Second Duet of The Queen and Essex

QUEEN

My lord of Essex!

Without taking her startled gaze off him, she waves away the Lady-in-Waiting, the Tiring-Maids, and the Maids of Honour. They curtsey and withdraw. Wisps of grey hair hanging round the Queen's face make her look old, pathetic and vulnerable: but it immediately becomes clear that she has not lost command of herself or of the situation.

QUEEN

Robin!

118

ESSEX
(*kneeling*)

Queen of my life!

QUEEN

What brings you here?

ESSEX

My love and duty.
Day and night from Ireland
I pressed on:
I had to see and hear you:
Madam, forgive me!

QUEEN

But what must I forgive?
Because you catch
An ageing woman unadorned,
You can be called unkind:
But the years pursue us
    And the rose must feel the frost:
And nothing can renew us
    When the flame in the rose is lost!
*She makes a tragic gesture, indicating her
appearance: then continues in the tones of a
sad old woman:*
You see me as I am.

ESSEX

Not less in majesty.
Oh give me leave to speak!

QUEEN

Oh pray, be brief:
The day's not yet begun.
Because you're here
When larks alone have right of audience:
Because you stand
Besprent with mud and hollow-eyed:
Because you're here
You must have need to speak.

ESSEX

Because the gale,
The gale of the world has caught me:
Because the world
Is full of lying tongues –

BOTH

Because the world
Must know the truth of things at last –

ESSEX

Madam, give me leave to speak –
You will forgive.
Tyrone I have bound to a truce,
But foes beset me now
Here in England, at home.

QUEEN

What foes are they?
Declare!

ESSEX

Madam, my foes are yours.
My place is at your side.

QUEEN

My foes are over there!
Tyrone is still untouched!

ESSEX

Ah! But the truce –

QUEEN

Were you not required
To break his power down?

ESSEX

Madam, at your command –

QUEEN

Is it at my command
That you are here?

ESSEX

That I am here –

QUEEN

Proves you unfit –

ESSEX

Proves me unfit!

QUEEN

Unfit! Ay, and more –
Proves you untrue!

ESSEX

I, trusty in arms,
The first to defend you,
Am I to be taunted?
O care, O heaviest care!
Against me, me,
They have turned even *you*!

QUEEN

You have failed in my trust,
You have left a wound
In a heart too fond,
In my heart!

ESSEX

Then let me heal you!
Ah, Queen of my life!

QUEEN

Dear name I have loved,
Oh, use it no more!
The time and the name
Now belong to the past:
They belong to the young,
And the echoes are mute:
Happy were we!

ESSEX

Oh, put back the clock
To the birth of our hope!
The chime as it rang
Told the hour when you gave
Of your grace, when I sang,
When my heart was the lute:
Happy were we!

QUEEN

Ah, Robin go now!
Eat, drink and refresh you.
Go, Robin, go!

*She takes up her looking-glass in her right
hand, and extends her left to Essex. He
kisses it, and goes slowly out, casting a long
look back at the Queen. The two Tiring-
Maids return to help her complete her toilet,
and the Lady-in-Waiting leads in the Maids
of Honour.*

LADY-IN-WAITING

My lord was early and abrupt.
Deign, Madam – allow our hands
To adorn our Sovereign in peace.
Come, Madam, come.

No. 4 The Dressing-Table Song

Lady, to your dressing-table
  Turn again, and there descry
Beauty resting, beauty gazing
  In her own admiring eye.

ALL

Gazing in a glass or glancing
Like Narcissus on his knees,
Beauty lives by her enhancing
And adoreth what she sees.

LADY-IN-WAITING

Tint with powder, touch with tincture,
  Lightly bind a wilful curl,
Fix about the waist a cincture,
  In each ear a moony pearl.

ALL

Lady, at your dressing-table
  With your ladies round you, gaze
Like a goddess in a fable
  At the glory of our days!

LADY-IN-WAITING

Pearl and ruby gleam and glisten,
  Dews bespangle open roses,
Golden gauzes, sun-rays dazzle
  All beholders!

*Her dressing done, the Queen waves all her
attendants away. As they go out in one
direction, she rises majestically to greet
Cecil, who comes in from another. / No. 5
The Entrance of Cecil*

QUEEN

Your presence is welcome, good elf.

CECIL

Burst in upon betimes unmannerly,
Was not your Majesty alarmed?

QUEEN

What fear is, I never knew.
But as we have authority to rule
So we look to be obeyed.

But why is he here? Tell me!
Tell what you know!
What say our faithful eyes and ears?

No. 6 Cecil's Report

CECIL

Tyrone is still a rebel
And Ireland not yet ours.
Not ours, but might be Spain's,
Might easily be France's:
For want of forthright action
He forfeited his chances.
And now it is September,
Too late for campaigning.
And now he's here in England,
With hangers-on unruly,
Armed, and out for trouble,
Madam – I see a certain danger.

No. 7 Discussion

QUEEN

Think of the waste!

CECIL

The waste!

QUEEN

Count up the cost!

CECIL

The cost!

QUEEN

Our orders defied!

CECIL

Defied!

QUEEN

There an idle force,
Here a rebel heart!

CECIL

A rebel heart!

QUEEN

In the eyes of the world
We now look a fool!

CECIL

But for a time!

QUEEN

Now is the time for the curb!

CECIL

The curb!

QUEEN

For the hand on the rein!

CECIL

The rein!

120

QUEEN

I trust him no longer!
Here is my command!

CECIL

Raleigh awaits your command!

No. 8 The Queen's Decision

QUEEN

From this hour my lord of Essex
Must be kept under guard.
My Lord Deputy hath defied me;
He flouted my orders.
The Earl Marshal of England
Is himself a rebel:
With his malcontent following
Brought back from Ireland
He endangers my country.
Close watch must be kept!

Ah, my faithful elf, it has come to this!
I have failed to tame my thoroughbred.
He is still too proud;
I must break his will
And pull down his great heart.
It is I who have to rule.

Curtain.

Scene Two. *A street in the City of London.
In front of a tavern sits a blind Ballad-
Singer, with a few old men grouped about
him; at his side a young Gittern player. A
boy, who acts as a runner for the Ballad-
Singer and brings him the latest rumours,
approaches him and whispers in his ear. /
Ballad – Rondo.*

OLD MEN

News! Give us the news!

BALLAD-SINGER

To bind by force, to bolt with bars
The wonder of this age
They tried in vain, they could not curb
The lion in his rage:
Great need had he
Of liberty,
And now hath bounded from his cage.

FIRST GROUP OF OLD MEN

What can he mean?

SECOND GROUP OF OLD MEN

Essex is out, at large!

ALL

Oh now we shall see
His followers arm,
And aldermen bolting
Their doors with alarm!

*The boy runs out. A rabble of boys marches
in, led by a man of Essex's following,
playing a drum.*

RABBLE

Now rouse up all the City
And join our gallant army
By noble Essex led:
And join us in our duty,
Make Cecil and make Raleigh
Both shorter by a head!
March along with us!

The rabble marches off, singing.

FIRST GROUP

What rabble is this?

SECOND GROUP

Are they rebels or mad?

ALL

Mere idlers and louts
Out to trouble the peace.

BALLAD-SINGER

Whenas the lion roams at large
And rages fierce abroad,
Then follow lesser brutes, a mob
That know him as their lord:
By day or dark
Like dogs they bark
And snatch the leavings from the board.

OLD MEN

Poor ravening knaves!
A boy runs mad
When for its bread his belly craves.

*Drums and turmoil are heard. Followers of
Essex seek with wild cries of "Saw! Saw!
Saw! Tray! Tray!" to enlist the citizens on
his side. As the tumult fades, the boy runs in
again and whispers to the Ballad-Singer.*

OLD MEN

News! Give us the news!

BALLAD-SINGER

The raveners grow bold, give tongue,
All thirsting after prey,
With noise they keep their spirits up,
As well indeed they may:
They can't foresee
What is to be,
The dreadful danger in their way.

OLD MEN

In mortal peril they must go.

*Cuffe, attended by young rebel officers,
appears, sword in hand, to harangue the
crowd.*

CUFFE

Citizens of London,
The Earl of Essex calls you!

FOLLOWERS

Hear the drums calling,
His enemies are falling!

OLD MEN

Nay, let him call!

CUFFE

Remember Cadiz,
But Spain is still intriguing!

FOLLOWERS

With plots, underminings,
And evil designings!

OLD MEN

He's right! He's wrong!

HOUSEWIFE
(*at window above*)

Hey, be off with your bawling!

FOLLOWERS

Down with the Council!

CUFFE

Let Essex save the Queen
From her false advisers!

HOUSEWIFE

Hear the ass braying!

CUFFE

To arms with Essex!

CUFFE AND FOLLOWERS

To arms for England!

HOUSEWIFE

To arms? To the gallows!
Thou rowdy! Sow's ear!
Thou slubberdegullion!
Thou eel's foot!
Rowdy cockerel!
Thou Pickthank!
Mongrel! Stool-pigeon!
Thou! —

CUFFE

The Queen is old,
Her power fails.
Essex must guard the Crown!

OLD MEN

That we should live into a season
When openly men practise treason!

CUFFE

Old fools! You still have time to learn
That those who deviate will burn!

HOUSEWIFE

Yah, Willy Wet-leg, you won't burn!

CUFFE

Slattern, I'll have your blood!

FOLLOWERS

Come forward!

CUFFE AND FOLLOWERS

Forward! March!

HOUSEWIFE

I'll damp your courage!
Take that, you wastrel!

The housewife leans out and empties a chamber-pot over Cuffe and his followers as they are marching off.

CUFFE AND FOLLOWERS
(*running out*)

Ah!

(*The onlookers laugh.*)

BALLAD-SINGER

Proud man goes strutting forth to slay,
  And brags with might and main,
But Goodwife Joan will jeer at him
  Till Pride itself is slain:
    It is her lot
    To keel the pot
And mock the hero home again.

HOUSEWIFE AND OLD MEN

It is $\begin{cases} \text{her} \\ \text{my} \end{cases}$ lot
To keel the pot
And mock the hero home again.

The City Crier with his bell is heard at the end of the street.

CRIER

Oyez! Oyez! In the name of the Queen! Be it known that Robert Devereux, Earl of Essex, erstwhile Lord Deputy in Ireland, having risen against the Crown and Realm of England, is this day proclaimed TRAITOR. Any man giving him aid, by word or deed, will be guilty of TREASON.

FIRST GROUP

Essex a traitor!

SECOND GROUP

Guilty of treason!

FIRST GROUP

There's trouble ahead!

SECOND GROUP

There always is!

ALL

The Queen, the Queen,
What will she do?

BALLAD-SINGER

In all his pride the lion roared
  And sought whom to devour,
But he mistook the time to spring,
  Mistook his pride for power:
    Down in the dust
    Soon fall he must,
For dire is the day, and dread the hour.

122

ALL

He asked for trouble
And trouble has come.
Trouble has come
And heads must fall –
We told you so!

The Ballad-Singer gives the boy a coin.

BALLAD-SINGER

Here, Harry boy, a groat –
Fill your belly, wet your throat.
There's work for you my boy!
Work! Work! Work!

The boy runs out.

Curtain.

Scene Three. *A room in the Palace of Whitehall. Cecil, Raleigh, and others of the Council. / No. 1 Prelude and Verdict*

RALEIGH

The trial now being over,
The traitor's malice ended –

COUNCILLORS

Essex is guilty and condemned to die!

CECIL

Councillors, take notice of my warning –
Beware of one thing yet!

RALEIGH

Of what?

COUNCILLORS

Essex is guilty and condemned to die!

CECIL

That is our verdict. In the Tower
He awaits the day.

RALEIGH

Wednesday is the day appointed!
He will see no later day!

COUNCILLORS

Essex is guilty and condemned to die!

CECIL

Beware of one thing yet!
The Queen may yet defer the deed.

RALEIGH

The day, but not the deed.

COUNCILLORS

Essex is guilty and condemned to die!

CECIL

She long delayed to seal the doom
Of the Northern Earls and the Queen of Scots:
She may delay once more,
Or even spare his life.

RALEIGH AND COUNCILLORS

Never! Essex can she not forgive!

ALL [16]

Essex is guilty and condemned to die!

The Queen enters. All kneel.

QUEEN

Let me hear the verdict.
Are you all agreed?

CECIL

May it please your Majesty,
The verdict was unanimous.

He turns to Raleigh and the Councillors.

RALEIGH

After trial the court has found
The Earl of Essex guilty of treason.

COUNCILLORS

Guilty of treason and condemned to die!

QUEEN

To die a traitor. Ah!

RALEIGH

Wednesday is the day appointed.

COUNCILLORS

Guilty of treason and condemned to die.

RALEIGH
(proffering the death-warrant)

Only awaits your royal hand
To ratify his doom.

QUEEN

I will not sign it now!
I will consider it.

No. 2 Cecil's Warning

CECIL

Madam, I humbly pray, do not defer
This dreadful duty,
Or the people will doubt
If the traitor is guilty
Or the Queen is safe.

QUEEN

Cecil, no prating
To me of my duty!
Silence!
The Council's dismissed!

They bow themselves out. The Queen paces up and down. / No. 3 The Queen's Dilemma

I grieve, yet dare not show my discontent;
I love, and yet am forced to seem to hate;
I am, and am not; freeze, and yet I burn;
Since from myself my other self I turn.

Raleigh steps boldly into the room.

Sir Walter, what now?

123

RALEIGH

Three persons, in humble duty,
Crave audience of their Sovereign.

*Behind him enters Lady Essex, her face
half veiled. She is supported by Lady Rich,
followed by Mountjoy. / No. 4 Trio*

LADY ESSEX, LADY RICH AND MOUNTJOY

Great Queen, your champion in a prison
    cell
Lies languishing. We come to plead for him,
To intercede for him,
Beseech your pardon, urge your need for him
Whose love and valour may still serve you
    well.

*Mountjoy leads Lady Essex forward. She
makes an obeisance to the Queen and sinks
to her knees.*

MOUNTJOY

To ask your mercy, Madam,
The Countess bows her head and kneels.

No. 5 Lady Essex's Pleading

LADY ESSEX

Too ill-advised
He greatly erred:
But let the father of my children live!

QUEEN

Hearken, it is a Prince who speaks.
A Prince is set upon a stage
Alone, in sight of all the world;
Alone, and must not fail.

LADY ESSEX

If he must die
I plead for my children,
His!

QUEEN
(gently)

Frances, a woman speaks.
Whatever I decide –
I have yet to name the day,
To sign his breath away,
His, that betrayed his Queen –
Whatever I decide,
Your children, Frances, will be safe.

*Lady Essex makes another obeisance,
covers her face with her veil, and steps
back.*

MOUNTJOY

His sister, Madam, begs to speak.
Deign to hear her pleading.

QUEEN

What! Tears from those bold eyes!
Tears from my Lady Rich!

No. 6 Penelope Rich's Pleading

LADY RICH

The noble Earl of Essex
Was born to fame and fortune,
Yet not his rank alone
Hath made his greatness known.

QUEEN

I gave him honour, gave him power –

LADY RICH

Greatly hath he served the State,
And armies follow him through fire.
Madam, you need him:
Let his greatness be.

QUEEN

He touched my sceptre –
Then he was too great
To be endured.

LADY RICH

Still great he would have been
Without the grace
And favour of a Queen!
Still great!

QUEEN

Woman! How dare you plead
For a traitor's life,
You, an unfaithful wife!

LADY RICH

No traitor he! Not he!

QUEEN

Justice hath found him so!

LADY RICH

Be merciful,
Be wise!

QUEEN

Be dutiful,
Be still!

LADY RICH

He most deserves
Your pardon –

QUEEN

Most insolent,
You dare presume!

LADY RICH

Deserves your love!

QUEEN

Importune me no more!
Out!

LADY RICH
(beside herself with rage)

God forgive you!
God forgive you!

QUEEN
(to Raleigh)

Give me the warrant!
I will sign it now!

As the Queen takes up a pen to sign the warrant, Lady Rich screams and throws herself into the arms of Mountjoy. The Queen signs the warrant and hands it back to Raleigh, who bows himself out. / No. 7 Epilogue / As Mountjoy leads Lady Rich and Lady Essex away, the stage darkens. The Queen is seen standing alone in a strong light against an indeterminate background. Time and place are becoming less and less important to her. [13]

QUEEN
(speaking)

I have now obtained the victory over two things which the greatest princes cannot at their will subdue: the one is fame, the other is over a great mind. Surely the world is now, I hope, reasonably satisfied.
(singing)
In some unhaunted desert . . .

THE VOICE OF ESSEX
(speaking)

I am thrown into a corner like a dead carcass and you refuse even to hear of me, which to traitors you never did. What remains is only to beseech you to conclude my punishment, my misery, and my life.

QUEEN
(singing)

There might he sleep secure . . .

Cecil appears standing near the Queen.

CECIL
(speaking)

The King of Scotland, may he not be told your Majesty's pleasure? Will it not please your Majesty to name the successor to your throne?

QUEEN
(speaking angrily)

I can by no means endure a winding-sheet held up before mine eyes while yet I live.

She dismisses him, Cecil bows and retires. The Queen, standing alone, directly addresses the audience.

QUEEN
(speaking)

I have ever used to set the last Judgement Day before mine eyes, and when I have to answer the highest Judge, I mean to plead that never thought was cherished in my heart that tended not to my people's good. I count it the glory of my crown that I have reigned with your love, and there is no jewel that I prefer before that jewel. Neither do I desire to live longer days than that I may see your prosperity: and that's my only desire.

Distant cheering. Near the Queen appears a death-like phantom of herself. It approaches and fades.

QUEEN
(singing)
Mortua, mortua, sed non sepulta!

Cecil appears near the Queen.

CECIL
(speaking)

To content the people, Madam, you *must* go to bed.

QUEEN
(speaking)

The word 'must' is not to be used to Princes! Little man, little man, you durst not have said it, but you know I must die.

CECIL
(speaking)

I wish your Majesty long life.

QUEEN
(speaking)

I see no weighty reason that I should be fond to live or fear to die.

Cecil disappears, and the Queen is alone again.

CHORUS [7a]
(off)

Green leaves are we,
Red rose our golden Queen,
O crownèd rose among the leaves so green!

The singing fades, and the Queen is slowly enveloped in darkness.

Slow Curtain.

Discography *by Martin Hoyle.* The enthusiast is referred to *Opera on Record*, ed. Alan Blyth, Hutchinson, 1979 for detailed analysis.

Conductor Orchestra/Opera House	*Britten* Royal Opera	*Davis* Royal Opera
Peter Grimes	Pears	Vickers
Ellen Orford	C. Watson	Harper
Balstrode	Pease	Summers
Keene	Evans	Allen
Swallow	Brannigan	Robinson
Auntie	J. Watson	Bainbridge

Disc	SXL 2150-2	6769 014
Tape	K71K 33	7699 089
Excerpts (disc)	SXL 2309	—
Disc US	Lon 1305/SXL 2150	6769 014
Tape US	—	7699 089
Excerpts US (disc)	Lon 26004	—

Sea Interludes and Passacaglia

LSO/Previn (with *Sinfonia da Requiem*)	ASD 3154 (UK) S 37142 (US - disc and tape)
NYPO/Bernstein (with *A Time There Was*)	76640 (UK - disc) 40-76640 (UK - tape) M34529 (US - disc) MT34529 (US - tape)
Philharmonia/Giulini (with *Variations and Fugue*)	SXLP 30240 (UK - disc) T-SXLP 30240 (UK - tape) Angel S 32615 (US - disc)
Royal Opera/Davis (with *Midsummer Marriage* exc.)	6527 112 (UK - disc) 7311 112 (UK - tape) 6527 112 (US - disc) 7311 112 (US - tape)

A **video recording** of The Royal Opera in *Peter Grimes* is also available. Elijah Moshinsky's 1975 production was recorded in 1981 with substantially the same cast as on the disc conducted by Colin Davis.

UK	US
VHS Cassette TVH 90 1712 4	Pioneer disc PA 82 008
Betamax Cassette TXH 90 1712 4	

Discography

At the time of writing no complete recording of *Gloriana* exists. All other major Britten operas, however, are available on issues from Decca (UK) and London (USA). It is planned that the 1984 ENO production of *Gloriana* will be recorded for gramophone, cassette tape and video tape/disc.

Choral Dances
    Aldeburgh Festival Singers   UEA 82015

2nd Lute Song
    Pears, Bream   GL 42752 (disc)
                                   GK 42752 (tape)
    Pears, Ellis   SXL 6788

Courtly Dances
    Bream   ARL3 0997 (UK)
                                   CRL3 0997 (US)

Symphonic Suite (with *Prince of Pagodas*)
    Bournemouth SO/Segal   ASD4073 (disc)
                                   TCC ASD4073 (tape)
                                   Angel DS-37882 (disc US)
                                   Angel DS-37882 (tape US)

Contributors

Peter Porter, Australian writer, poet and broadcaster, has published several anthologies of poetry.

Stephen Walsh is music critic for *The Observer* and a lecturer in music at University College, Cardiff.

Buxton Orr, composer and conductor, teaches at the Guildhall School of Music and Drama.

Michael Holroyd is the author of biographies of Lytton Strachey and Augustus John.

Rupert Hart-Davis, author and former publisher, has edited numerous collections of letters and written a biography of Hugh Walpole (1952) and a memoir, *The Arms of Time* (1979).

Christopher Palmer is the editor of the forthcoming *Britten Companion* (to be published by Faber).

John Evans is the Research Fellow for The Britten Estate.

Bibliography

Of the general surveys of Britten's music, *The Music of Benjamin Britten* by Peter Evans (London, 1979) may be most highly recommended. There is also Patricia Howard's earlier study of the operas only (*The Operas of Benjamin Britten*, London, 1969) and Eric Walter White's *Benjamin Britten: his Life and Operas* (London, 1983). Introductory essays about working with Britten, the texts of all the operas and some of the original designs, are contained in *The Operas of Benjamin Britten* (ed. D. Herbert, London, 1979).

Several short biographies have appeared (notably that by Alan Blyth, *Remembering Britten*, London, 1981), and there is the fascinating illustrated biography by Donald Mitchell and John Evans (*Benjamin Britten, 1913-1976: Pictures from a Life*, London, 1978). Donald Mitchell is currently working on the authorised biography. Lord Harewood's autobiography contains reminiscences of a lifetime of association with Britten, and vivid descriptions of the first nights of both operas in question (*The Tongs and the Bones*, London, 1981).

Peter Grimes is the subject of Sadler's Wells Opera Book no. 3 (ed. Eric Crozier, London, 1946) and of a Cambridge Opera Handbook (ed. Philip Brett, Cambridge, 1983), in which the composer's own brief introduction to the opera is reprinted.

Although there are no books about *Gloriana*, David Cairns devoted an essay to it in his anthology *Responses* (London, 1973).

Apart from *Elizabeth and Essex* itself (reprinted London, 1981), Michael Holroyd's *Biography of Lytton Strachey*, (reprinted London, 1981), throws fascinating light on the author's self-identification with the characters. Unfortunately, the *Autobiography of William Plomer* (London, 1975) does not deal in any depth with his collaboration with Britten, although it mentions his introduction to the Bloomsbury set when Strachey was at work on *Elizabeth and Essex*, and contains certain amusing anecdotes concerning the first night of *Gloriana*. An anthology of Plomer's writings, *Electric Delights*, which includes a reminiscence of the first night of *Gloriana*, 'Let's Crab an Opera', was made by Rupert Hart-Davis (London, 1978).

Peter Pears as Grimes at Sadler's Wells in 1945 (photo: Angus McBean)